Praise for
One Moment Please

'*One Moment Please* is a gentle wake-up call, beautifully written and so timely and necessary.'
— Dr Jean-Philippe Lachaux
Cognitive Neuroscience Research Director, INSERM
Lyon, France

ONE
MOMENT
PLEASE

Also by Martina Sheehan and Susan Pearse:

Wired For Life:
Retrain Your Brain and Thrive

Please visit: www.hayhouse.com.au

ONE MOMENT PLEASE

It's Time to Pay Attention

Copyright © 2015 by Martina Sheehan and Susan Pearse

Published and distributed in Australia by: Hay House Australia Pty. Ltd.: www.hayhouse.com.au
Published and distributed in the United States by: Hay House, Inc.: www.hayhouse.com
Published and distributed in the United Kingdom by: Hay House UK, Ltd.: www.hayhouse.co.uk
Published and distributed in South Africa by: Hay House SA (Pty), Ltd.: www.hayhouse.co.za
Distributed in Canada by: Raincoast: www.raincoast.com
Published in India by: Hay House Publishers India: www.hayhouse.co.in

Design by Rhett Nacson
Typeset by Bookhouse, Sydney
Edited by Margie Tubbs
Author photo by Tanya Love Portrait

All rights reserved. No part of this book may be reproduced by any mechanical, photographic, or electronic process, or in the form of a phonographic recording, nor may it be stored in a retrieval system, transmitted, or otherwise be copied for public or private use—other than for "fair use" as brief quotations embodied in articles and reviews without prior written permission of the publisher.

The author of this book does not dispense medical advice nor prescribe the use of any technique as a form of treatment for physical or medical problems without the advice of a physician, either directly or indirectly. The intent of the author is only to offer information of a general nature to help you in your quest for physical fitness and good health. In the event you use any of the information in this book for yourself, which is your constitutional right, the author and the publisher assume no responsibility for your actions.

CAT'S IN THE CRADLE Words and Music by HARRY CHAPIN and SANDY CHAPIN, Copyright © 1974 (Renewed) STORY SONGS, LTD., All Rights Administered by WB MUSIC CORP., All Rights Reserved, Used By Permission of ALFRED MUSIC

ISBN: 978-1-4019-3865-9
Digital ISBN: 978-1-4019-3383-8

18 17 16 15   4 3 2 1
1st Australian edition, March 2015

Printed in the United States of America

Dedicated to all the people we withheld time from during the writing of this book. Rest assured that you didn't lose our attention for one moment.

Contents

Foreword by Pam Grout		xi
Introduction		xv
1	The World's Most Threatened Resource	1
2	Attention is a Gift	12
3	Precious	28
4	Attention Muggers	41
5	Attention Thieves	58
6	Space Invaders	76
7	The Great Escape	94
8	Wise Investments	113
9	Start with One Moment	130
References		145
About Mind Gardener®		149
About the Authors		151

Foreword >

Can you imagine Newton even noticing a falling apple if he was dashing from one meeting to the next anxiously barking instructions on his cell phone? Would Shakespeare have finished The Tempest *if he was battling the trolls on his Twitter account?*

—*Martina Sheehan and Susan Pearse*

I live a charmed life, partly because I get up every morning and proclaim, 'Something amazingly awesome is going to happen to me today.'

One beautiful Saturday in September 2014, one of the awesome things that happened to me was meeting Martina Sheehan and Susan Pearse, the authors of this book, at a Hay House writers' conference.

You know that warm feeling you get when you immediately connect with someone who minutes before was a total stranger? That feeling that reminds you that, in Truth, in the Big Picture, we're all one, we're all friends pretending not to know each other. So even though I live in the centre of the United States and Martina and Susan live beside a gorgeous ocean in Australia (no, I'm not bitter), I feel completely connected to and buzzed by the energy of these two geniuses.

As it turns out (coincidence, I've heard, is God's way of staying anonymous), they had, just that morning, finished the manuscript of this book. And because we did feel (or I did) like soul sisters from another if not planet, at least country, they asked if I'd be willing to endorse their book.

I thought, of course, I was doing them a favour. But then I read the manuscript (thanks to the very attention-stealing culprits they talk about, it was a full three or four weeks later) and I realised they were the ones doing ME a favour.

I need this book as a reminder—to pay attention, to be more present, to more fully love the people in my physical life. Like everyone else on this crazy planet, I had practically handcuffed myself to my smart phone. I was shocked to learn the world currently has more cell phones than working toilets and like Martina and Susan point out, I'd invited mine "to travel in my pocket and sleep by my bed". This marvellous wonder of technology had turned into this huge Frankenstein-like attention suck.

I was so busy dutifully checking my email, my Twitter updates and my Amazon reviews that I thought were so important to the success of my just-launched book that I'd forgotten to notice the crimson red and orange in the last full moon. I was working so hard to answer emails, to respond to fans, to keep on top of interview requests that I, more often than I care to admit, was completely ignoring the guy who shares my bed every night.

– FOREWORD –

This book, *One Moment Please,* is the cold splash of water, the reminder I need. I'd like to thank them for reminding me of what's truly precious. And my partner, Jim, would like to send flowers.

Way to go, soul sistahs!!!

—Pam Grout, *New York Times* best-selling author of *E-Squared*

Introduction >

It's often said that you teach what you need to learn yourself. There is no doubt that our own personal search for better ways to navigate life's twists and turns led us to the work we do, and revealed our true purpose: to wake up the world. Because there is an excuse every day for being mindless instead of mindful, for switching off when we should be paying attention, for dwelling on what might have been rather than facing what is, and for letting our minds wander rather than being fully present.

Our lives changed once we understood what it really meant to be present. Actually, that's not true. Understanding what it means doesn't change anything. Our lives changed once we *started* to be more present. The difference between understanding it or talking about it or thinking about it, and actually doing it is like night and day. The moment you bring your attention fully into the present is the moment you connect with life.

You probably know this too, but if you're like so many others, us included, you need constant reminding and encouragement.

So for the last fifteen years we've been teaching people how to literally and practically be present in all the moments that make up a life. And as a consequence, we continue to learn how to be present in our own.

But we learnt more writing this book, *One Moment Please,* than at any other time in our journey. We started with a simple message and you'll find it in these pages: attention is being misused and abused more than ever before, and it's time we saved it. We thought we would write the 'how to' book on attention, but as it revealed itself, something more important emerged.

We realised that attention is the most precious gift. We learnt that spending time is no substitute for giving attention. We experienced the vibrancy of a life lived fully. We felt the deep pleasure of making clear and conscious choices. But we also learnt that withholding attention is a destructive act, and that the breakdown in the ready flow of attention is the end of care. And we saw more clearly than ever before that there is no time to waste. If we want to live in a world where it is possible to find true happiness, experience real meaning, connect deeply and love fully, we must all act now to revive the dying art of paying attention.

So this book is a plea to you, a wake-up call to the world. It's unapologetically direct, and some of the messages might be tough to hear. But if you see yourself in these pages, don't waste a moment on regret or guilt. We were personally challenged by what this book said to us, and by the time we'd finished writing it, we had changed the way we thought about many things, and the way we were parenting, working and living. By the time you have finished reading this book, we believe your life will be changed too.

– INTRODUCTION –

May you be inspired by the wonder your attention reveals in the world around you, awakened to the things that matter to you most, blessed by the care that flows when we pay attention to each other, and rewarded by living in a world where attention opens the door to wisdom, compassion and peace.

1 The World's Most Threatened Resource

WAKE UP > Sitting in the front row of the auditorium, I feel the anticipation build inside me. Within minutes, I'll be addressing the students of my old high school at their annual speech night. The room is overflowing with thirteen to fifteen-year-olds coming to the end of their junior schooling years, and proud parents and grandparents sit by their side. The uniforms may have changed, but nearly thirty years ago I had the same speech night in the same auditorium. I can see myself in every one of their faces. But life was so different back then. Memories flood in of those carefree years, and my mind wanders off to visions of schoolyard games, passing notes at the back of the classroom, walking home with friends . . .

I'm woken from my reverie as the school principal calls my name, '. . . so join me in a warm school welcome!' and a thousand sets of eyes follow my approach to the podium.

How do I tell them in twenty minutes what has taken me half a lifetime to learn? Would I have understood it, if I'd been told at that age? As I speak, I'm aware how unique this event is. Three generations sit at my feet. The oldest may have escaped the worst of the looming threat, but they are touched deeply by the turmoil left in its wake. Those my age are living with its effects daily, but their children are growing with the crisis as if it is the norm. Could I warn them?

Looking down at their young faces, I feel an overwhelming urge to plead with them. I feel like I am trying to save a younger version of myself. And this is what comes out of my mouth:

When you hear your teachers and parents telling you to pay attention, you may treat it as a joke. But if you take one thing away from my talk, I hope it will be this: start learning to pay attention now, otherwise when you get to my age you will be in serious, serious trouble.

Attention is the most threatened resource on the planet today. It is being misused and abused more than ever before. If you've ever juggled a phone under your chin, responding to someone on the other end while continuing to work on your computer, you're a culprit. If you ring a friend to share the latest gossip, with no thought about whether they have something more important to do at that moment, you're also guilty. If you sit in a meeting pretending to listen, but worrying about all the other things on your to-do list, you're offending too. But those are minor misdemeanours these days. The attention police (if they existed) would let you off with a simple warning for such careless acts. Lucky too, or we'd all be in "attention prison" by now.

But maybe we are; a prison not of physical walls that separate us from life, but one just the same, one just as isolating. One where we've lost the connection with each other, where our days are filled with activity but no meaning, where we cannot see beauty, smell fresh air, hear laughter, or experience joy.

'I feel like I'm losing my mind.' It was a clear autumn morning, but this outwardly successful leader was lost in a fog of confusion. 'I can't remember things, I can't get focused, and small issues are really worrying me.' The story is too familiar. A similar refrain can be heard from growing numbers of small business owners, teachers, lawyers, leaders, students, retirees and parents. Our generation is not just witnessing a simple trend of encroaching busyness. Something more significant is happening—more than just the stress and frustration of a busy life. Our generation is now describing a sense of overwhelming disconnection and despair: 'I feel numb, like nothing I do has any meaning.'

Life's beauty is found in the small moments. But without a stable and pure thread of attention to connect you to them, experiences are tarnished, memories fade, and it all passes by in a blur. It's not until love walks out, the grind of work wears you down, sleep rarely visits, and life has lost its colour that you stop and wonder what you've missed. Surely this is not how it's meant to be.

A GIFT > Attention is the most glorious of human gifts. It is the radar that navigates you safely through the world. But it is so much more than this. Attention is the thread that connects you with life. It can catch the mere hint of danger in the air. It can draw you in close to a loved one. It can reveal the beauty of the day. It can breathe life into your hopes and dreams. It is a stream that flows constantly, and every experience, memory, belief and emotion you have ever had, started with the kiss of attention.

Attention is as real and tangible as the light that surrounds you and the gravity that holds you in place. It is a physical force, mysterious but familiar nonetheless. You know when you are in its presence, and you know when it is being withheld from you. You know when your attention is stable and healthy, and you know when it is stretched and strained. The many worlds where your attention can wander seem as real as this one here now, but they exist only as wisps of smoke that vanish as soon as attention moves on. Attention is a birthright to be honoured, precious but more fragile than we have ever realised. And it is only now, as it becomes more threatened by the pace of the modern world, that we are beginning to realise that it is attention that brings us to life.

Distraction breeds disconnection, and disconnection breeds despair. A full life does not demand more of anything but attention. But this may be asking the one thing many people are finding hardest to give.

FATAL DISTRACTION > The early warmth of a spring afternoon greeted a father, as he left work and drove to a day care centre to pick up his eleven-month-old son. On arriving at the centre, he was told that no-one had dropped the boy off that morning. In a gut-wrenching moment of realisation, the father and centre staff rushed to his car and found the young child lifeless in the back seat.

But before you ask, 'How could this happen!?' or judge the parents involved, you should know that these incidents are not as uncommon as you might hope. The sad fact is that fifteen to twenty-five children of loving and otherwise attentive parents die in the US alone every year, from just this sort of momentary lapse of attention.[1] In one case, a father who had recently been laid off from his job dropped his older daughter at day care, but as he was driving the baby to a different location, he received a phone call about a new permanent job. This captured his attention and proved to be a fatal distraction. Preoccupied with problems at work, distracted by an interruption, overwhelmed by busyness, affected by stress, mindlessly following a routine, or tricked by a change in routine, one important task on the to-do list was missed, with haunting consequences.

A momentary lapse of attention, something many of us experience daily, is all it takes to change your life. A lapse of attention is a moment of your life lost, completely and irreversibly. If you're lucky, it only results in misplaced keys, a forgotten name, a bad golf shot, or a wrong turn on the way home. But what happens when you spend half your day disconnected from life? Because apparently, that's become the new norm. The average person spends 47 percent of their time "mind–wandering", doing one thing but thinking about something else.[2]

Not all minds that wander are lost,[3] but increasingly, they are. Teachers who have dedicated decades to educating young minds confirm that the challenge involved in holding the attention of their students is unprecedented. 'There's always been mind wandering,' one remarked at a recent forum, 'but twenty years ago, kids would at least wander onto related topics that would benefit their creativity. These days, we struggle to even **get** their attention.'

Even a wandering mind is short-changed when your attention is under threat. Ragged and distracted attention has no time for deep exploration, and opts instead for shortcuts; the shorter the better. It has been suggested that the average attention span has halved in the last ten years.[4] Can you imagine Newton even noticing a falling apple, if he was dashing from one meeting to the next, anxiously barking instructions into his mobile phone? Would Shakespeare have finished *The Tempest*, if he was battling the trolls on his Twitter account? Darwin would not have pondered the amazing patterns that emerge from the diversity of life, if his long walks were filled with worries about what other people thought of him, or how they would react to his ideas.

UNHAPPY DISTRACTION > 'How are you?'

'Busy. You?'

'Busy.'

'That's good. You want to be busy.'

Do you? There comes a time when every busy person has simply had enough. It is no coincidence that rates of anxiety have risen in almost perfect proportion to the decline of the idle arts. Trading off the quiet and slow journey that attention will naturally take through your inner world and your outer experience during idle time, for the quick hit of just one more box ticked, is a bad deal.

When your attention is flooded, it's working overtime to do even its most basic job of navigating you safely through life. It doesn't stand a chance of going deeper and connecting you to the moments that make life the amazing experience it is meant to be. And the consequences are all too apparent: mindless mistakes, loveless relationships, inattentive service, exhausted parents. In a workshop recently, a participant revealed the dread she feels as night approaches, knowing that she will be entering

- 6 -

the battleground of her noisy mind. Reduced quality of sleep and the inability to switch off are now just taken for granted, but they should be taken as a warning . . . they reflect a deeper problem.

People report feeling less happy when their mind is wandering than when they are paying attention to what they are doing, and this finding holds true even when their mind is wandering to pleasant things.[2] The World Health Organisation reports that depression is the leading cause of disability worldwide;[5] and the burden of depression and other mental health conditions is on the rise globally. Every study on youth anxiety levels screams out an urgent plea for action. More information, more access, more choice, more change, more uncertainty, more expectation, more, more, more . . . Robbed of the indulgence in deep exploration and slow contemplation, where once you found inspiration, self-awareness, purpose, love and joy, you are instead forced to skim the surface of life. There you find the natural companions of inattention: ignorance, forgetfulness, assumption, complacency and frustration. Paying attention is a dying art, and we're paying the ultimate price.

ATTENTION IS THE CURRENCY OF CARE > Even the most simple dictionary definition reveals that the act of paying attention is an act of care. It means that you regard someone or something as interesting or important. Above all others, you have chosen to tend to them in this moment, for attention can only truly be given to one thing at a time. Attention is the medium for the exchange of everything in your life that is worthwhile. Without it, you cannot give or receive kindness, compassion, love, guidance or support. Without it, you cannot experience beauty, inspiration or wonder. Without it, we are disconnected not only from each other, but also from ourselves. The break-down in the ready flow of attention is the end of care.

When you give generously of your attention to others, they thrive in its warm glow. But when it is withheld, they suffer. As you lose the capacity to give full attention to life, you are not only the architect of your own disconnection and despair, but also the instrument of others' pain.

An elegant lady in her seventies lined up to order her drinks. There was a thrill in her voice as she chatted with the barista. She was a local, and he was asking about the young boy at her side. 'My family is visiting for Christmas and this,' she proudly explained, 'is my grandson. He is twelve years old and we're on a date!'

She happily collected her order, but anyone watching would have witnessed her joy turn quickly to sadness as, for the next twenty minutes, her young grandson played his computer game. Her few attempts to start a conversation elicited mere nods, she received no eye contact, and with every passing minute, her radiance faded ever so slightly. She did not protest and she did not intervene in his play. She appeared at a loss in the face of this unexpected intruder in their midst. Robbed of the very thing she had so looked forward to experiencing with her grandson, she somehow maintained a pleasant smile, but the heavy burden of resignation had replaced the invigorating spark of pride. She seemed more alone than those sitting without a companion.

It's not that care is dead, but the things that most deserve the transforming gift of true attention are being sidelined, in the battle to deal with an onslaught of attention muggers, thieves and grabbers. Attention is busy getting on top of tasks, working

THE WORLD'S MOST THREATENED RESOURCE

through worries, juggling conflicting priorities, re-running regrets, and gorging on an endless flow of junk. There's little return except the short-lived relief of ticking something off your to-do list, but attention deserves more. The currency of care brings the things that it touches to life. It is a slow-burning fuse that moves from person to person, growing in strength as it is shared, and bringing light to us all.

For a moment she hesitated. He was not usually home so early. Maybe they could get dressed up and go out to dinner. But no, she hadn't finished those last few niggling tasks, and she turned back to her computer.

Attention is being wasted on the meaningless, leaving very little for the meaningful. If you want a full life, you must pay full price. When you short-change life by giving only fragments of attention, you must accept only fragments in return: fragments of information, fragments of meaning, fragments of experience and fragments of connection. Just as your heart can become starved of oxygen and vital nutrients from clogged and hardened arteries, your life becomes starved of meaning and vibrancy from a daily diet of busyness and bad habits. The resulting "life dis-ease" shows up as frustration, stress, difficulty in focusing, loss of memory, insomnia, burnout, anxiety, purposelessness, disappointment, disconnection and even death. You might be surprised to hear that these seemingly complex life challenges could find their genesis in something as simple as not being able to pay attention, but there is a clear and direct relationship between healthy attention and a harmonious life.

THE WAY BACK > It's tempting to dump this problem at technology's door, but that would be oversimplifying it. The boom in mobile technology has certainly thrown into stark relief how fragile attention really is. It has undoubtedly accelerated us to this point in history. But it only highlights that the power of attention has been taken for granted for far too long. The genie was already out of the bottle, and switching off technology alone will not revive this threatened resource. In the absence of mobile devices and "always-on" communications, we are only too accomplished at abusing our own attention, and frittering it away on worries, what-ifs and wasted thoughts.

As the sense of being overwhelmed builds, the effort to shake it off grows stronger. There's a growing realisation that it's simply not possible to fit more in, but some still hold out hope that a pause in proceedings will give them time to catch up. Others try to run away, literally or mentally. Clarity, stillness and peace of mind seem elusive, and unprecedented numbers of people, from all walks of life, are on the march, searching for a way to reconnect. Yoga and meditation classes are flooded with executives and professionals, hoping one hour of mindfulness will balance sixteen hours of mindlessness. The most popular stress relief methods are watching television and listening to music. Sure, these techniques offer relief for a short time, but only because they distract your attention from the things that capture, devour and exhaust it throughout the day. They are a short-term escape, but no lasting cure.

While it seems appealing to close up shop and build a dam wall to hold back the world, your goal should not be to bunker down and selfishly guard your attention. Our world will suffer if we all lock this powerful force away. We need it to flow freely again, not blocked and filtered, but pure and strong. When you give it wisely to the things that matter most, and save it from

-THE WORLD'S MOST THREATENED RESOURCE-

those things that will wastefully consume it, the returns flow back to you through a virtuous cycle that nourishes all in its path. The gift of attention is only precious when given generously, gently and intentionally. The only way back to a full connection with yourself, with others, and with the magic unfolding in every moment, is to revive the dying art of paying attention.

The majesty of this world, the magic of being alive, and the wonder in life's moments never lose their lustre. But we lose sight of this when attention fades. You were given the gift of attention so you could experience life—and the exciting truth is that it takes just one moment to save it! One moment of full attention can quieten your busy mind and soothe your tired body. One moment of full attention can bring colour to your world, fill you with awe and make your heart soar. One moment of full attention can nurture a child, save a relationship, reveal a solution or change the world. These moments remind you that attention is a gift and, no matter how harshly you have treated it, a flickering flame waits patiently for you to reignite it.

One moment is all it takes to revive the dying art of paying attention. One moment is all it takes to connect with life and experience it in full colour once again.

2 Attention is a Gift

THE ELIXIR OF LIFE > In a neonatal unit of a city hospital, special cribs holding newborn babies line the walls. A plastic bubble of tubes, IV lines, and UV lights is their first home—all essential for saving these babies, who were born well before their time. But despite the power of all of these machines, there is one force greater than them all: the power of their mothers' attention.

Kangaroo Care is used around the world to help premature babies survive and thrive. Skin to skin contact with a parent, even if just for a few moments a day, is transformative for the newborn baby. But for a mother, these moments are not just about skin contact. These moments are time to give full attention. With a clear mind, nothing exists except the touch of soft skin, the smell of her new baby, the sight of her greatest love. It's a moment of absolute presence. I know, because I have been one of those mothers. I know that attention gives life.

A dose of attention is an essential source of health and happiness at every stage of life. Through it pours love, care, and support. A new romance glows brightly, as a couple overflows with attention given and received. The warmth, enthusiasm and contentment is so tangible that friends and family often know love is on the scene before the story breaks. The glow of new love fills every nook and cranny. You listen intently to every word that comes out of your new love's mouth, and every movement they make is fascinating. It is attention that is the true bond of love.

Doctors with a caring and nurturing style have been found to shorten the recovery process for their patients, proving again that attention is medicine for the soul. These studies found that patients who experienced the greatest relief were those who were given the most care, and the more care people received, the better they recovered.[6]

Emotions are highly contagious, but it is the gift of full attention that enables emotions to flow freely between people. The person who gives attention generously, without allowing it to be coloured or tainted, draws others to them. This physical force has the potential to right the world.

The gift of attention draws you back to places where you experience great service, genuine care, and strong connection: the cafes, the restaurants, the place you get your car serviced, your hairdresser, or your dentist. They're the ones who build their business on attention, creating a solid foundation that bricks and mortar could never provide.

To be exposed to the attention of others can literally extend life, and to be withdrawn from it causes pain, stunts mental performance and increases the chance of disease.[7] You can feel someone's attention leave your side. Their eyes fade and the warmth of connection is replaced by an empty chill. You are left alone.

WITHHOLDING ATTENTION IS A DESTRUCTIVE ACT > The sad real-life experiment on orphans in Romania hit world head-lines, after the leader, Nicolae Ceausescu, was deposed in 1989. Shocking images poignantly revealed the crippling effect of leaving children untended. They were fed and changed, but deprived of individualised affection. We learnt that attention delivers more than a child's physical needs. The nourishment of attention is tangible, and it is the key to unlocking a child's full potential. Without attention, they cannot blossom and grow. Withholding attention is not a neutral act; it is a destructive one. Neglect does more than rob a child of their chance to thrive. Attention's absence leaves room for destructive emotions to breed: fear, stress, anxiety and pain.

Consider brain images that reveal the effects of a primary caregiver's nurturing behaviour on the development of a child's hippocampus.[8] The hippocampus is a region of the brain, important for learning, memory and responding to stress. Those children for whom nurturing care and support was withheld, experienced 10 percent less growth in hippocampal volume. Their vulnerability to anxiety and early-onset depression increased, and their learning outcomes were negatively affected. Giving the gift of attention is like turning on a tap. Through it, you can shower a child with love, guide them to learn, and provide them with a sense of security that allows them to attend to the important work of growing and flourishing.

Your physical presence alone is not enough to perform this life-giving act. And your time is not the right measure either. It is the gift of your attention that nourishes most deeply.

The answer to why our need for attention is so deep and enduring can be found in one of the most basic functions of the brain. Human evolutionary success is tied to our ability to live successfully in tribes, as social animals. Relatedness enables us to work together to beat the odds and not only survive, but also thrive. The slightest sign of rejection is a warning, for to be left out of the group is to be left to fend for oneself. Receiving the gift of attention from another is the first step to being included, but its lack is the first sign of danger.

And so today, many tens of thousands of years after humans first banded together to beat the odds, our highly evolved brain still associates a lack of attention to be, at best, a challenge to be overcome and, at worst, a dire threat. Either way, the brain activates its stress response, forcing you to remedy this threat as quickly as possible. Your brain will allow you to turn yourself to nothing else until you have dealt with this threat. Children clamber to get your attention; employees repeat their concerns until they feel they have been heard; lovers nag and accuse just to get a bite in an otherwise complacent relationship; pre-pubescent boys tease the girls in an experiment they do not yet understand; and bullies push and shove, searching for what is cruelly withheld from them elsewhere in their life.

NEGLECT IS PAINFUL > Attention's counter is disregard, carelessness and neglect. Sometimes, withholding attention is an intentional act, undertaken for the purpose of causing great pain. More often, it's committed unintentionally. But this makes it no less hurtful because, either way, withholding attention halts the flow of essential and life-giving nutrients for the spirit. It's like turning off the tap, switching off the light, or sucking the air from a room. More than emptiness, this void is experienced as a physical ache.

At a morning tea break, a manager told of his recent experience with attention, or the lack thereof. His area was under pressure and one of his colleagues asked, 'How are you going?' In hindsight, he realised this was probably just the rhetorical exchange so common in a work day. But just then, it was the question he needed someone to ask, and he opened up with, 'I'm really struggling.' His colleague, head down, folder and mobile phone in hand replied, 'I'd better get to my next meeting,' and disappeared out the door. 'It's not that I needed him to stay and talk it all through with me, but his inability to even look up, put a hand on my shoulder, or say "I can see that" was more upsetting than any of the problems I had been facing. I felt really alone.' The brain registers rejection in the same place that it registers physical pain,[9] meaning the experience of being ignored really **is** like a slap in the face.

THE MOST VULNERABLE > It is the youngest and oldest in society who pay the highest price, as attention becomes a threatened resource.

'I realise now that I missed a lot when my children were young. They seemed to grow up when I wasn't looking, and suddenly they were off living their own lives. I don't see them as much as I'd like.' This colleague's story was reminiscent of the lyrics from the 1974 song 'Cat's in the Cradle' by Harry Chapin:

My child arrived just the other day
He came into the world in the usual way
But there were planes to catch and bills to pay
He learned to walk while I was away . . .

In a world where the precious gift of attention has become more rare and endangered, we have set off a chain reaction, for which progressive generations pay a higher price. Inattention plants the seeds for more inattention; neglect grows, and loneliness is our legacy.

I've long since retired, my son's moved away
I called him up just the other day
I said, 'I'd like to see you if you don't mind'
He said, 'I'd love to, Dad, if I can find the time
You see my new job's a hassle and the kids have the flu
But it's sure nice talking to you, Dad
It's been sure nice talking to you
And as he hung up the phone it occurred to me
He'd grown up just like me
My boy was just like me.

Ageing adults with a larger network of friends, outlive those with the fewest friends by 22 percent. Exposure to attention is vital for health and longevity, and isolation has been identified as a risk factor for premature death, on par with smoking and high blood pressure.[5]

Sadly, many people report feeling that they become invisible to younger people as they age. On her 100th birthday, she was sitting in the busy studio with friends and family all around, as the two TV hosts invited them all to sing *Happy Birthday* on the live morning show. The signal was given and a busy assistant rushed on set carrying the birthday cake. The tiny centenarian's face lit up when she saw the cake and, as it was placed in front of her, she looked up, searching to make eye contact with the assistant to show her gratitude. But the connection was never made. The assistant delivered the cake, but not the true gift.

The last few decades have seen an increase in the elderly living alone, particularly in western societies. This is not all bad news because, for many, it is a choice and reflects the growing opportunities for healthy independent living. But as economies grow, extended families become fractured. Even the best efforts to stay connected can come under pressure: a weekly video call to a parent drops to a fortnightly phone call, then a monthly SMS. After a life full of experiences, relationships, dreams and challenges, to face death alone must be the most daunting challenge of all. At the end of life, as the physical body begins to reject food and oxygen, the vital force of attention can be absorbed until the very end, soothing the spirit. No-one should die without this gift.

EMPTY TIME > We often accuse time of being the culprit for stealing life's precious experiences, but it is the absence of attention that degrades relationships and robs life of meaning. Time is an empty vessel without attention at the helm.

The senior lawyer working four days a week spends Thursday with her eighteen-month-old son and three-year-old daughter at a coffee shop, at the park or in the playroom at home. But she checks her emails constantly. She is nervous that her colleagues consider her part-time status to be a bit of a joke, and she wants to prove them wrong. 'I can't let my clients suffer, so I just make sure things keep moving. But I'm not prepared to give up this one day with my kids while they are young.' She later admitted this was the toughest day of the week for her. She felt guilty about not being at work, and she felt guilty about rushing her kids through the day. Deep down, she was happy to return to the office each Friday. But that also made her feel guilty. This was not the life she had imagined.

Parents under pressure are convinced that what they are withholding from their children is time. Whether you're a mother holding down a busy job or a separated father who only gets two days each fortnight, it's easy to make this mistake. And it's an incredibly disempowering one. When your best efforts to find more time prove futile, it's tempting to compensate with the things you **are** able to provide: toys, games, material goods without true meaning . . .

> *My son turned ten just the other day*
> *He said, 'Thanks for the ball, Dad, come on let's play*
> *Can you teach me to throw?' I said 'Not today*
> *I got a lot to do', he said 'That's okay'*

What if you've been getting it wrong? What if the very thing your loved ones most need and want is not the one thing that is out of your reach, but the thing that is right at your fingertips? What if you are looking in all the wrong places, but overlooking the only thing that really matters? What if time doesn't matter, but attention really, really does?

Think they're the same thing? You couldn't be more wrong. A day spent together, but disconnected, is empty—even harmful.

What lesson does your child learn, when their efforts are over-looked and their ideas are ignored? It may surprise you to hear that studies show mothers spend more time with kids today than they did in 1965; but being in the same room doesn't guarantee a connection.[10]

As she unpacked the dishwasher, squeezing one more task in between returning home from work and preparing dinner, her nine-year-old chatted about her day. Moving quickly across the room, putting plates in cupboards and cutlery in drawers, she responded, 'Uh-huh, that's good,' a few times. 'So what do you think?' her daughter finished. 'Okay, time to do homework!' she replied, completely oblivious to the important question her daughter had finally worked up the courage to ask.

Attention is not measured in seconds, minutes, hours or days; it is measured by fullness. A moment of clear full atten-tion, given generously and without condition, will connect, nourish and transform. But as long as you hold on to time as your measure, these moments of full attention are delayed until "the time is right". You don't need to wait until the weekend, an annual holiday, a birthday or other special event, to give this most precious and life-changing gift. This message is particularly important for time-poor parents. Instead of wasting the short time you have together by filling it with activity, entertainment and distraction, try filling it with simple, pure attention. You can give it right now, switch it on at any moment, and offer it at any time. You will be surprised how quickly a child's needs are satisfied by this generous gift.

A single dad had almost given up. 'They come to me every second weekend. I can tell they don't want to be here. I hate it that they spend more time with their step-father than with me, and I think I'm losing the battle. I always take them to fun parks or the beach. There are ice-creams, toys, movies, and I've got all the games they love on my tablet. But they start fighting with each other or get that whinging tone in their voice, and I just don't know how to handle it. I end up raising my voice, they retreat, and by Sunday everyone is glad it's over. People keep telling me I'm a good dad, because I spend this time with my kids and I never let anyone interrupt our time together. I keep all the normal weekend tasks out of the way, so they can feel like they're the most important thing in my life. What am I doing wrong?'

'Why don't you try this? Before you pick them up next weekend, tell yourself that the most precious gift you will ever give them is your full attention. Then do just that. Don't predict what will happen; just start and see where it takes you.' He was dubious about this experiment, but he was also ready to try something different to save his relationship with his children.

At 9am on Saturday morning, his SMS came through. 'Last night was amazing! We built a cubby house in the lounge room and they read me a story. Now they want to spend the day helping me in the yard. They've never been this much fun! It works!!'

'I'm glad. Now stop sending messages and pay attention!'

The following Monday, he was exuberant as he shared his story. 'I finally realise how much I've been missing. I thought I had to entertain my children, but now I can see that what they needed from me was much more profound, but so much easier. They had been fighting to get my attention through all the barriers I had set up. When I stopped trying so hard and just listened, that feeling I had been searching for was there.'

ARE YOU WATCHING? > Children are expert at ramping up their "attention-seeking behaviours" when they sense you are drifting. It starts with chatter, then questions, then repetition, then silliness and, finally, if nothing else works, naughtiness. That usually gets a response; harsh words or punishment are a price they're prepared to pay to satisfy their need. You've finally bestowed on them the much sought–after prize, and a connection is made. This connection is crucial for learning, understanding, encouragement, motivation and the security of belonging. But is any attention better than no attention?

A study on how employees respond to the attention of their leaders suggests that it is.[11] Not surprisingly, an employee's level of engagement drops significantly if the leader focuses on the employee's weaknesses rather than strengths. But the surprising finding was how disengagement dramatically worsens, when an employee is ignored. It seems that negative attention is better than no attention at all.

'Hey, guess who this is?' he joked, as he mimicked someone constantly checking his phone, when he was supposed to be listening. The others laughed and nodded, knowing immediately who he meant. The person on the receiving end of the joke was their boss. Years of withholding attention had taken its toll, and he was left with a team who didn't respect him—a team not prepared to go the extra mile for him. He was aware of their disengagement, but he didn't understand it. He tried all the usual responses: reward schemes, social functions and motivational speakers. But he rarely attended, often walked out to take a call when he did come, or delegated the activities to someone else. But you can't delegate attention, and you can't buy it in. People will put up with a lot of nonsense, but once they

- 2 2 -

give up trying to get your attention, you've lost them. Personal agendas, minimal effort, and lack of accountability are the legacy of a leader who has not invested in the one resource that fuels every successful business: the currency of care.

And so it goes for relationships of all types. Attention is a deep need, rarely considered in its own right. In a world increasingly starved of attention, it's easy to settle for a poor reflection of the true gift, or to make a hasty grab for a scrap. In the search for even just a glimmer of it, partners stay in abusive relationships; workers remain in jobs that drain their self-confidence; vulnerable young people fall prey to those who mean them harm; and whole countries follow charismatic madmen. When what should be a gentle thread of connection is loaded with the burden of expectations, emotion or bad intent, it becomes instead a harsh rope pulled tight with cruelty, malice or abuse. This deep need for attention drives perpetrators and victims alike. But when reaching out for attention becomes striking out, the quality of the attention that is exchanged is coloured with anger and fear, and all care is lost. This is no longer the gift of attention, your true birthright.

It's a trap of the brain—a misinterpretation made by the heart—to think you must accept the unacceptable, just to gain a glimmer of attention. And it's also a mistake to think you must revert to poor behaviour to get someone's attention. Deals like this will never deliver. If you ache for love, then offer and accept attention without expectation, judgement or agenda. Attention should be clear and transparent, not coloured green with envy or red with anger. True care and love, compassion, understanding, acceptance and meaning will only flow through an unadulterated stream of attention.

DO YOU CARE? > We're all guilty of neglect from time to time. Partners use the silent treatment to force a reaction from their mate. Teenagers frustrate their parents with the response, 'Whatever!' But in a world where attention is under threat, it is not surprising to see increasingly obvious, but often oblivious, breakdowns in the flow of this life-giving resource. At close glance, a romantic dinner reveals two individuals absorbed in sharing their night on Facebook, rather than with each other. An elderly man holds the door open for a group of approaching businessmen, and they brush past him without as much as a nod of thanks. The light turns green but the car in front does not move, and drivers behind punch their horns in frustration.

These common daily occurrences are surprisingly difficult to shrug off. Such small acts should not feel so offensive but, when you remember that the exchange of attention is the only meaningful currency that exists between us, withholding attention when it might naturally be expected actually **is** offensive. It's like wearing a big sign that says, 'I don't care!' More than any other response, this makes your brain scream out in rage. It's time we accept that we don't just need oxygen, food and water to survive, but the constant flow of nourishing, clear, untainted attention as well.

'I only had affairs because I felt ignored at home. She was so absorbed in the kids and her career, and I never felt like she really noticed me. For so long I tried to do things that would make her turn to me with bright eyes and tell me she thought I was wonderful. I wanted to get the feeling that being in her life made a difference to her in some way. But nothing seemed to really work and, after a few years, we were just living in the same space. It was friendly enough, but distant. I should have left; but by then I thought there was something wrong with me, and probably no-one would want me. The affairs were ways of proving someone noticed me, but they never made me feel better about myself. In fact, I feel like I've lost not only my marriage, but myself in the process.'

MISSED MOMENTS > Moments are like sliding doors. You might miss a moment, or maybe you won't. And it can make all the difference not only in that moment, but in the way life unfolds for years to come.

Today I'm going to tell her. She made this promise to herself as she walked home from school. *I can't face the bullies alone anymore. But what if she thinks I'm not tough enough? What if she thinks less of me, because I can't stand up for myself?* But the pain she was experiencing, from being victimised at school, was now greater than her resistance to telling her mother the truth.

'Mum, what's there to eat?' she asked, as she walked in the door. 'Oh, grab an apple,' came the reply from the other room, where the noise of the vacuum cleaner nearly drowned her out. 'Mum, where's the pencil case I left behind today?' 'Where you left it on the kitchen bench.' She was now cutting vegetables for dinner and they were in the same room. Now was her chance. 'Mum . . . ?' Just one more request from a teenager; she could feel her frustration rise. But just as she was going to burst out with, 'What's wrong now?' she sensed something that she couldn't really describe. So she put down the knife and gently asked, 'Yes dear, what is it?'

WORLD CHANGING > A decline in the valuable resource of attention accounts for growing hostility and conflict. The first piece of advice most people will offer when you're having a problem with someone—whether it be partner, colleague, client, neighbour or friend—is, 'Why don't you get together and talk about it?' The power of a face-to-face exchange is undeniable. To put a face to a name and experience body language, emotions, and nuance builds a bridge far stronger than the virtual connection we rely on far too much today. People will work harder and longer in the service of those who they have personally met, than they will for the faceless beneficiaries of their efforts.[12]

Some of the most powerful peace projects are grass roots efforts that focus on building connection between individuals "on the ground". Once you pay attention, really pay attention, without judgment or criticism, to who someone really is—what they feel, how they think, and why they act the way they do. This deeper level of understanding builds a foundation for lasting connection.

On Christmas Day in 1914, German, British and French soldiers left their trenches to play football together. They did so after hearing each other sing Christmas carols. The simple act of listening, of paying attention only to the sound of familiar songs, triggered connection, even through the horrors of war. Connection exposed unity, not difference; and, one by one, they ventured into no man's land to share food and eventually play football together. A growing mood of "live and let live" gave rise to more and more truces through the coming year. Senior officers became so concerned by the declining appetite for fighting, they replaced soldiers in an effort to break down this connection. And by 1916, the use of poison gas finally turned the tide. It became easier to view the other side as less than human. Attention was withdrawn, and fighting became the only focus.

In this world where attention is assaulted daily, the last thing the world needs is for any of us to hold it back or lock it away. Attention grows healthy through use, by giving it to the things you care for most, and by letting it feed on the flourishing exchange that comes from these moments. Holding a bit back in reserve may sound sensible, but all it does is disconnect you from life. This world needs attention to flow strongly and freely, towards the things that help us all to thrive.

My young niece watches me as I turn back to my computer. She had been happily drawing at the table while eating afternoon tea, so I thought I was safe to check my emails again. But she didn't miss my subtle move, and started chattering on to me about something. I made what I thought was a suitably positive response, and the chatter continued on. But the discomfort of short-changing her like this finally gets to me. It is all too obvious that attending to my emails means I am simply not hearing her. I turn my chair and look right at her with a big smile, and immediately her face brightens. Attention once more connects us. Her whole spirit lifts, as if we were meeting after a long time apart.

3 Precious

WAKE-UP CALL > Sometimes you do not realise how precious something is until you're just about to lose it. Even if you're not happy with the state of your attention right now, you've still got to love it for what it can do. Life offers countless opportunities and experiences, asking only for a moment of attention as payment. When at its best, attention is the merchant of magic, trading in the only currency accepted at the doorway to a full life. But too often, you spend a penny here and a dollar there, frittering it away until there's nothing left for life's big stuff.

All too often, people approach the challenge of reviving the dying art of paying attention like they are engaging the enemy on a battlefield. No matter how frustrated you have become with your attention, it is not your enemy, it is your best friend. Or at least it is trying to be.

A Letter from Your Attention

Dear friend,

I don't think you know what it is like for me to live with you.

When you wake up, the first thing you do is grab that wicked little smartphone (why do they think it's so smart?). Before you've even put your feet on the ground, I am overloaded with junk from Facebook (when are you actually going to believe one of those nice quotes and change your life?). I'm left wondering about those questions your boss emailed through overnight (didn't we deal with those same questions last week?). I'm distracted by your friend's constant relationship dramas (there is nothing left to say about this!) and now you want me to remind you if today is Wednesday or Thursday (I have no idea either . . . !).

Then your body runs off without me. You had me rehearsing that conversation with your boss while you were in the shower, but I wish I could have just enjoyed the warm flowing water. You forced me to listen to "drama friend" on the phone, while you made the sandwiches (I hope you remembered to pack the fruit in the lunchbox this time). You dragged me back through your to-do list five times before you left home, but it still seems no clearer. Where are we? Oh, stuck in traffic. What! You forgot the folder with the print-outs!! How could I have seen it! Now I'm focused. Quick turn left, then right and stop here with your hazard lights on. Run through the gate; don't trip on the cat! There it is on the bench. Damn, knocked over the new pot plant on the way back out. I don't know why he bought that stupid thing. Forget it, just get back in the car and go! Now the kids will be late. Push out in front of that nice person, smile and wave. Have fun, kids, see you later. No!! Please don't pick up that phone. Can't we just sit here quietly and enjoy the rest of the trip to work in peace?

Do you remember the time we watched that amazing sunset at the beach? It's the last time I recall feeling truly at one with you. For just a short time, the only thing that mattered was the sky's shifting colours, the call of birds on their way to their nightly perch, and the smell of the sea as the breeze lifted. For a moment we were together, and nothing else intruded. When you stirred, you gently sent me off on a wonderful journey to a place you had not visited for a long time. It was the vision of your life in which you were doing what you loved, and I pictured you so strong and happy. But the moment you broke the stillness with that familiar thought "I can't", you have not been treating me well.

It's been eight months since then, and I am exhausted.

Since you gave up on your dream, you've also given up on me. I've been trying to navigate you back there, but every time we get a glimpse of it you drag me back through an endless loop: what if it doesn't work, why you can't do it, what would people think . . . I've been on high alert for the past eight months, trying to stay one step ahead of all the problems you've been contemplating. And now you're blaming me and complaining to your friends that I keep you up all night. Can't you see that my travels are dictated by you? You've been sending me on too many quick trips to dark places and dead ends. All I can bring back from there is what I find: negativity, fear and frustration.

I've become addicted to junk thoughts: the false high of busyness, the quick fix of gossip, the adrenaline rush of stress. But this diet is killing me. I'm on edge all the time, jumping at shadows. You seem to think that giving me a break means walking away from your desk and grabbing a cup of tea. But that's when you give me even more to mull over! I'd rather be sitting at the desk, focusing on simple tasks, than roaming in the wilderness that beckons when there is nothing useful to do. I know you think it's my fault that the first thing you do in the morning is grab your mobile phone to check messages, worry about the day's to-do list, re-run the problems from yesterday, and rehearse conversations that might (but probably won't) happen.

I'm so sick of wandering around trying to make deep connections and find rich experiences, but always coming up short and disappointing you. If you could just let me stop for a moment, I'm sure the ideas and inspiration, meaning and purpose, hope and happiness you once had are still within reach. But I've got a lot of bad habits to break first.

We are far more powerful when we work together, but I'm getting weaker every day. I don't want to break up with you, but I feel like we're already so disconnected from each other. Please wake up before it's too late.

Your precious gift,
Attention

Attention is a limited commodity. When it is soaked up by the trivial, the destructive or the irrelevant matters that tease and tempt it, little is left to cultivate and care for the things that deserve your special interest. It's easy to overlook the early signs of damage: lapses in memory, lapses in patience and lapses in care, all indicate that attention is beginning to fragment and fray. If they go unheeded, short lapses become lengthy losses.

For most people, the wake-up call is a crisis, a realisation, or a period of pain during which the cracks they have been deftly avoiding abruptly open into chasms, and the fall is inevitable. Suddenly you find yourself in a world where you have inadvertently given over your most precious gift to things that hold you back, hold you down or hold you prisoner. And those things have grown stronger.

The phone cut harshly through the stillness of 2am. 'Sorry for calling, but I didn't know what else to do.' Through sobs, her story unfolded. It had been a dark period since she left her husband five months ago, but guilt, doubt and fear had become her constant companions, taking over most relentlessly in the quiet of night. 'I can't stay awake when I'm out with friends, but I can't sleep when I'm at home. I try to drown out the noise of my own mind with the TV, especially when I'm going to bed. I hate being alone with myself. It's like sitting in the front row of a horror movie, and I cannot stop re-running all the negative and hurtful things that happened.'

You cannot run away from your attention. This thread is tied to you irrevocably, and where the other end lands creates the tapestry of your life. If you attach it tightly to dark moments of hurt, you design a life of regret and sadness. If you leave it floating loose in the wind, you become the victim of chance, vulnerable to things that invade your attention or steal it for their own ends. But if you reach out, as a curious child does to a passing balloon, holding on with wonder and joy, you become the architect of every moment.

After fifteen minutes or so, she had the courage to confront the quiet night, and hung up the phone. But it took many more months before she was able to see that, in her effort to battle the dark thoughts that had inhabited her mind, she had only been driving herself more deeply into despair. 'I wondered why

I couldn't think of anything else. Why couldn't I extract myself from this awful nightmare? If I found myself laughing with a friend, I would suddenly realise I'd forgotten my worries, and then they would come flooding back. Then I finally got it. Despite all the other wonderful things that I could be giving my attention to, I'd developed a really bad habit of dragging it back over and over again to this sad story. It was like an old song stuck on repeat, and I finally realised only I could choose a new one.'

THE POWER OF CHOICE > The capacity to resist urges, impulses, temptations and distractions, and to instead make conscious choices about where your precious attention will be invested, is one of the most reliable predictors of future success and life satisfaction. Children who show signs of what is commonly referred to as "impulse control" early in life are, years later, better adjusted, better at handling stress, and less likely to abuse drugs. They have better relationships and earn more money than those who struggle with this control.[13] It's the child who realises that their limited pocket money will only stretch to a couple of tasty treats, who chooses wisely and savours deeply. The choices you face each day aren't as simple as candy, but the act of conscious choice is just as important. Faced with multiple devices with dancing images and constantly updating gossip, a world of uncertainty to wonder and worry about, endless lists of tasks waiting to be done, and constant interruptions, distractions, wants and needs, are you the puppet or the puppeteer?

The faculty of voluntarily bringing back a wandering attention, over and over again, is the very root of judgment, character and will . . . An education which should improve this faculty would be the education par excellence.

WILLIAM JAMES, AMERICAN PHILOSOPHER AND PSYCHOLOGIST, 1842–1910

Attention is a tool of raw power. Learning to use it wisely, selectively, and with discipline, is the skill that will carry you through a full and fulfilling life. But untamed, it will run in circles and bolt at the slightest scare. When you learn how to harness your attention, cherish it as precious, treat it with care and use it well, you become the master of your destiny, navigating through life's twists and turns with the power to choose your path, rather than being dragged defenceless down every dead–end alley.

Mobile technology can slay impulse control with one strike. You'll see marked changes in behaviour, the first time anyone (of any age) is introduced to a device. 'We'd really like to get a tablet, because there are some great apps for preschoolers. Our cold London winters make it hard to be outside, but this will help to keep him stimulated on days when we're stuck inside.' The grandparents were visiting for Christmas, and it had been a wonderful few days with the family. Their grandson was three and a half, a delightful child who greeted them every day by running at full pace with arms wide open and a long, 'Heeeelllooowwww!' A short visit to the shop proved that he would be a natural, as he tapped and flicked the tablet on display. Before they even finished the transaction and left the shop, he had graduated a few levels on the colour recognition app. They parted at the bus and all looked forward to one last day together, before the annual visit would to come to an end.

The next morning the grandparents eagerly arrived at the house, craving one more traditional loud and affectionate greeting. But all was quiet, and they found their grandson sitting on the floor with his head down, drawing shapes on his tablet. 'Come on dear, say hello,' urged his mother. But it required the removal of the tablet from his sight before he lifted his head, and then it was with a howl of dismay and real tears. In a few short hours, this attention wizard had won over another apprentice. It was only the discipline adopted by his wise parents that saved his impulse control from crumbling completely and being lost forever. But one thing was lost that day: the last heart-warming exchange of pure loving attention.

But your impulse control remains vulnerable throughout life, and it's not only external intrusions that can divert your precious attention. Your own thoughts can lead your attention on a merry chase, taunting and tempting it further and further away from where it is most needed.

'I think something's burning!' he called from the other room. She jumped up suddenly, remembering the toast she had put into the griller. 'Just as I put it in, I remembered a message from a friend earlier in the day, asking if she could borrow my suitcase. So I went to get it out of the cupboard, and found that it still had some books from my last trip inside. I was sorting through those, then went to the bookcase to put them in their place. I was casually pulling old books out, when the burning toast call came!'

We all have days when it's easier to maintain attention and stay focused on what matters. And we all have days when it's not. If you cannot leave your mobile phone behind without feeling a gnawing sense of anxiety, that's a sign your impulse control is struggling. If you jump immediately to respond to a new request without taking a moment to consider its relative importance, your impulse control has not even been given a chance to have its say. But it's not just your ability to resist the urge to act. Impulse control is, more importantly, the ability to **recognise** the urge, and to consciously direct your attention to what matters, rather than have it stolen by things that don't. If you can resist the urge to look at an incoming SMS while you are in the middle of an important conversation, but still wonder all the while who it might be, what has happened, or whether you are missing something important instead of really listening, then your impulse control is a façade.

HEALTHY AND HAPPY > Like all the other vital forces that bring you to life, attention is a constantly flowing stream, always there to bring you to the world, and bring the world to you. It snakes through your environment gathering sights, sounds, smells, tastes and sensations, carrying them to your awareness. It re-emerges from your mind with perspectives, opinions, responses, emotions and questions. Healthy attention is not static and fixed. It pulsates with movement, free to turn to stimuli from any direction, and capable of being directed quickly and deeply to the places you want it to go, whether out in your surroundings or within your own mind. If you take a moment to notice, you can track the movement of your attention, just as you can feel your heart beat and your breath rise and fall.

Healthy attention is wide open to the world, gently scanning and lightly connecting to a myriad of moments. Healthy attention responds to your wishes, by turning effortlessly toward the things you choose. Healthy attention can switch smoothly in the face of a multitude of distractions, investing just enough in each to respond effectively. Healthy attention heeds the alarm sent by fear and stress, but then decides calmly on the wisest path. Healthy attention can remain steady on one thing of great importance, without missing something more important that might emerge. Healthy attention is energised by engagement, but can also rest peacefully. When invested wisely, healthy attention grows even stronger and healthier.

But this finely-balanced force is fragile. It takes very little to knock it from its equilibrium. Left untended, it is an easy victim. The brightest and loudest stimuli are irresistible without impulse control, and your attention can be easily captured and stolen without this guard at the gate. Unhealthy attention is flighty, too anxious to be still for even a moment. Unhealthy attention is coloured by judgements, expectations and assumptions, unable to clearly recognise reality. Unhealthy attention grasps for more and more stimulation and squirms uncomfortably in the face of a quiet, empty moment. Unhealthy attention is indiscriminate, seeking fleeting rewards over those that last. Unhealthy attention is lazy, preferring old worn ruts to the challenge of a new adventure.

There are so many things fighting for a piece of this most precious resource, for it is a prize worth more than gold. What you focus on grows, and each drop of attention has the power to nourish whatever it touches. If you are not happy with the things that are growing in your life, you need look no further than where your precious attention is flowing.

If the only thing you use your attention for is to push blindly through the white water washing through your life, then it will get better and better at that. But it will avoid at all costs the slow deep dive below the surface, where things are clear and still. And the opposite is also true. When your attention becomes comfortable with the slow pace of a quiet life, a sudden sprint through a flurry of hectic distractions is exhausting. If its only diet is the junk fed through a TV or computer screen, it will recoil at the nutritious meal offered by a weekend in nature. If it revels in worries and thrills to the hyper-alert state of impending doom, the parallel world where all is good and things turn out well is a fantasy it simply ignores.

Attention is designed to connect you with what's most important. It's the only thing that ever will. But you must jump in the driver's seat and work gently to bring it back home. It is only when you treat attention as your most precious gift, that you will come back together in a marriage that will bring you joy, peace and harmony. Loving your attention means walking hand in hand together. It means introducing it to those things that you care for most. It means protecting it from things that will damage it. It means treating it like it's the most precious thing in your world.

MY FAVOURITE THINGS > 'That is the most amazing wardrobe!' We were receiving the grand tour through her new apartment, and she had kept the best till last. 'I had it designed specially. It fits every bag, and I can see all the shoes in one glance. Of course, there's plenty of room for more too. It makes life so much easier. And this drawer here holds all the polish, brushes and cloths that I use to keep them looking so new. It's my Sunday afternoon ritual. I find it therapeutic.'

How is it that a $200 pair of shoes can receive better treatment than your attention, the precious but fragile thread that connects you with life? You would not be alone in admitting

- 3 8 -

that you treat a favourite pair of shoes (or your car, or your fine china dinner set, or your bicycle, or your wine collection), better than you do your own precious attention.

When you consider something to be precious, you hold it dear, appreciate it, and show it respect. You give it regular care and maintenance, keep it in a special place, and protect it from thieves. You speak of it with pride and affection, and show great interest in how it works. You certainly wouldn't wait until it is frayed and tattered before taking action. But for most people, it takes the near loss of this fragile gift to reveal how precious attention really is.

Of course, it's easier to take care of a pair of shoes or a new suit. They come with instructions, so you have some warning that certain things will damage this precious item. Wouldn't it be great if your attention came with such a tag?

Care Instructions
This item is fragile.
If used incorrectly, it may weaken or fade.
If used properly, it will become stronger and brighter.
Do not expose it to more than one source of information at a time.
Let it rest for a moment between every use.
Clear it at least once per week in fresh air and sunlight.
Beware that it will take on the colour and shape of whatever it is exposed to.
This item is easily stolen, so do not leave it exposed.

Unfortunately, we didn't receive these tips before we started using (and probably misusing) our attention. Most of us would instead be searching frantically for the "Troubleshooting" section in the instruction book about now. 'I think my attention span has shrunk! Is there any way to stretch it to fit again?' or 'My attention is stuck on the "fast & noisy" cycle. How do I switch it back to "slow & quiet"?' or 'My attention has been overexposed to dramas. Can I ever wash them out?'

You can't keep your attention in the box you bought it in. It's not a shiny toy to display on the shelf. Attention is for using and using well. Sometimes it will spin out of balance, but just gently set it right again. Attention is precious, but only when it is doing what it came here to do: connecting you to life and spreading care throughout the world.

A WORD OF CAUTION > Attention seeks connection and assailants lay in wait, pouncing not only on a fragment left unattended, but intruding without conscience, anytime, anywhere. Attention: muggers, thieves and invaders live right under your nose. In fact, they live in your pocket, within your most trusted circle of friends, and inside your own mind. You'll trip yourself up with a world of imaginary stories. Even your best friends and family members can be attention thieves, stealing a moment to feed themselves at your expense. And yes, mobile technology is the most obvious attention assailant.

4 Attention Muggers

A MUGGER IN DISGUISE > In San Francisco on the west coast of the U.S., the first chill of autumn was in the air, as a dozen or so people travelled on the city's light rail system. Among them, a twenty-year-old student with a promising future stood by the door, preparing to exit. As he went to step out of the carriage, he was shot in the back of the head—a random victim in a meaningless shooting. When video footage was released, it showed the gunman clearly raising his gun and pointing it across the aisle a number of times, making no attempt to hide his movements. But no-one saw him. Every commuter that night was engrossed in the activity on their smartphone or tablet, oblivious to the danger in their midst.

Sight and hearing are by far the most dominant senses, and it is mainly through those that threats are revealed. But they are also the senses that modern mobile technology recruits to tease and tantalise you. With your eyes and ears captivated by an endless show of colour, sound and movement, your mind can be miles away, mesmerised by another story, oblivious to the one unfolding around you.

Mobile technology is one of the most accomplished and expert attention burglars on the planet. It operates in broad daylight, but is well disguised as a friend and ally. No need to wait for an album's release; download the single now while you're travelling home from work. Weather tomorrow? I'll check it for you. What does that word mean? I'll tell you. She's got a new boyfriend? Let's check him out on her page.

The mobile world at your fingertips promises ease, efficiency, knowledge, entertainment and connection. It pilfers a moment here, another there, always convincing you that it is a seer of all, and that what it offers is important, essential, meaningful and necessary. Sometimes the promise is fulfilled, but more often it trades in shiny jewels that prove worthless on second glance. You invite them to travel in your pocket and sleep by your bed, and they will forever change the way your attention engages with the world.

WHEN THE FLOOD CAME > 'When I first became a manager, an inbox was a physical tray sitting on my desk, not an icon on my computer. The things my manager wanted me to read appeared in my in-tray each morning, and I decided what needed to be distributed to the members of my team. Even when the company got email, I still seemed to spend most of the day meeting with colleagues to progress matters, working at my desk to develop strategies and policies, and talking with team members to answer questions and help keep things moving. I don't remember ever feeling under pressure from too many emails, or calls on my mobile phone.' She was talking about the changing face of the office when she was a senior manager in a very large business.

'Compared to now, it felt like someone turned on a tap a few times each day. A bit of information flowed in, then the tap went off and you could empty the pool before it filled again. Now the tap is jammed in the "on" position and we're drowning!'

Warnings have been heralded through the ages. The first reference to the assault on attention can be found as early as the 1st century AD, when the philosopher Seneca said, 'the abundance of books is distraction.' And even before the floodgates of the modern information age were opened, Herbert A. Simon, an economist, wrote in 1971, 'A wealth of information creates a poverty of attention.'

But the tipping point really came decades later, when this wealth of information went mobile. No longer tethered to the desk, or dependent on others for information, mobile technology delivers the world to your fingertips. In its few short years among us, its most remarkable feat is to have convinced us to surrender our most precious resource day after day, and to do so willingly, even eagerly.

Ding, ding! We were halfway down the shopping aisle and halfway through a conversation about tonight's dinner, when the SMS alert echoed from her handbag. 'It's Trish. She's sent a photo of the christening outfit to your email and wants to know what we think. Can you open it up and we'll call her back?' I realised then how hard it is to stem the constantly rising tide. This was not a gen Y mobile native, but a seventy-four-year-old grandmother receiving a message from her seventy-three-year-old friend. They were like serpents dancing to the snake charmer's tune; the spell was so strong, that my refusal to open the email

- 4 3 -

there in the shop was seen as disruptive behaviour. Indignantly she capitulated, 'Well, I'll have to send Trish a message explaining why I can't get back to her for another hour.'

Later, I reminded her of a time in history when we were so much more respectful of the connections in front of us, rather than the ones that stridently intruded. 'I remember being a small girl, at the counter of a large department store with you. We were next in line to be served and, just as we moved forward and you started speaking, the phone rang and the shop assistant took the call. It was like someone had pulled the rug out from under you. You made it very clear to her that the right thing to do was serve the person who had patiently waited their turn, not let the person on the end of the phone effectively jump the queue. I feel like it was one of the first lessons on attention that I really remember.' The light bulb went on. 'It's exactly what I did today, isn't it? There's just something about these mobile phones. What is it?'

They're entertaining, enticing, addictive, comfortable, exhausting, promising, constant, frustrating, rewarding and tormenting all at once. They reach out and take hold of you through your most dominant senses of sight and hearing, and their ability to jump to the front of the queue is unsurpassed. Bewitched by someone's version of real life, neatly framed in black and silver, you don't want to miss a thing. They use the brain's own strengths as weaknesses. Whether it's the fear of missing out on a vital message, the seduction of salacious gossip, the anonymity of keeping the eyes down, the pleasure of an instant reward, or the grip of habit, mobile technology is the ultimate attention mugger. When you're connected to so many stories unfolding all over the world, things can change quickly.

It's intriguing and colourful. It's life without the boring bits. It fills your mind with tasty morsels to chew on all day. Real life with its mundane, repetitive ordinariness seems pale by comparison. No wonder attention surrenders so easily to such an amusing hijacker!

LOSING CONTROL > Mobile technology is a formidable foe, a Trojan Horse that entered as a welcome gift, then silently unleashed mayhem. We are already bombarded by the equivalent of 174 newspapers full of data each day, and we generate even more than that, sending it back out into the world for others to consume.[14] It is predicted that we will soon be downloading more than twenty-four hours of media on mobile devices every day. More people across the globe have access to mobile phones than working toilets, so maybe it's not surprising that we send three times more SMSs each day than there are people on the planet. When it takes an average of two minutes to respond to an email, how do you cope when you are receiving over one hundred a day? And this is only expected to increase! Impulse control is the first casualty in this battle to win a piece of attention, a prize that has been mined like precious metal for time immemorial.

A story doing the rounds recently about a manager would be funny, if it wasn't such a clear indicator of the problem. He puts his phone on silent, but he must be worried a message will come through and he'll miss it. He's got this habit of constantly pushing the home button. Last week he was meeting with a team member at a local coffee shop, and the action has become so habitual that he was pushing his finger onto his wallet instead of his phone. The staff member was trying not to laugh at him. When he realised what he was doing, he just shuffled things around and kept talking. And of course he immediately pushed the button again!

Impulse control is the guard at the gate. When it's too weak to do its job, attention leaks out of every nook and cranny. Attention muggers broke down the door and let the flood in, and the tide just keeps rising. The mobile device is so much more than a neat toy. It's the face of a new social order, the peddler that promises true social connection. It has become more than a phone, and on any day just look around and you will see people with their heads down and eyes glued to social media.

'Did you see them?' the stranger asked. Startled, she looked up from her phone. Eager to share the beauty with friends at home, she was posting a picture of the clear blue ocean on her feed. 'The dolphins!' he continued, enthusiastically pointing out to the right. And there they were, four dolphins within metres of the boat, frolicking in the ocean and putting on a show for everyone to see. It was a very rare sight for that time of year and she'd almost missed it, buried in the promise of connection elsewhere, but disconnecting herself from the only real moment she could have right now.

Attention simply can't cope with simultaneous streams of information, or simultaneous points of focus. Despite popular opinion, you are at your most productive, not when you are multi-tasking, but when you engage in one thing at a time.[15] Chunking information into bite-sized pieces, then chewing through it all before taking the next bite, is the polite way to feed your brain.

JUMPING THE QUEUE > Mobile technology cracked the code for jumping to the head of the queue. You may argue that it connects you in a way you've never been connected before, but the question remains: have you hitched your precious and limited attention to the things you care for most? The answer is likely to be "yes" and "no". A reassuring SMS from your son, telling you he arrived safely at his destination on his first big overseas trip, is priceless. The ability to download a document at the airport, so you can send back edits before it goes to print, eliminates a last-minute dash from the office to make your flight. Being able to chat face-to-face with your grandkids, who live half a world away, is a joy unmatched by a photo and a phone call.

The question is not whether these amazing tools are valuable. They are not the enemy, but more like an eager friend who wants to be sure you don't miss any of the fun. The question is not whether they belong in your life, but whether you are the servant or the master.

Corporate mum made it just in time to watch Friday afternoon swimming lessons at the local pool. Her five-year-old daughter waved excitedly when her searching eyes landed on this familiar shape rushing through the door. But there was clearly something else going on somewhere else that made mum draw her mobile phone out as soon as she sat down. Physically present but preoccupied, she was oblivious to her little girl's face turning constantly for a nod of approval, a sign of encouragement, a simple gesture of love that could only reach her if mum looked up.

'Your daughter is just adorable.' The well-timed comment from the mother sitting nearby was enough to bring her back. In that moment, her eye caught the open and loving gaze of her daughter, as she spluttered to the end of one more lap across the shallow end. This was enough to remind her why she had made the choice to be here, rather than the office. During the last ten minutes of the lesson, mum was leaning forward, smiling and clapping whenever her daughter looked to her, and the little girl became more adventurous with each turn. It was as if she felt her mother's hands holding her safe. This is the power of attention.

So much of what technology draws your attention towards is not aligned with your true interests, with what is most important to you, or with what you hold dear. Instead it invades your attention, a mugger in disguise. If you face its onslaught without the capacity to make conscious choices about the what, the when, and the how, it will quickly leave you more disconnected than ever.

MISSING LIFE > There have always been distractions, but these attention muggers have changed the game completely. Mobile devices bring the head down, requiring your eyes to lock on and your attention to narrow in. Attention should return with something useful or meaningful from every journey, but when it's captured by a device, it has no chance of picking up the signals around you.

And this is why they are so deadly. In the time it takes to send an SMS while you are driving, you can cover the length of a football field. It's like driving with a blindfold on. It might take only a few seconds, but it's enough to kill yourself, or an innocent stranger, or both. Studies on the reaction times in cars show that talking hands-free is worse than being under the influence of alcohol.[16] People are walking into fountains, walking into each other, and walking into the path of oncoming vehicles. Attention has never met a foe like the mobile device, one that has so successfully undermined attention's most fundamental role: alerting you to danger.

- 48 -

Police will tell you that recent years have seen a rise in needless death and injury from the simplest of acts. It not that we always paid attention so perfectly before, but inattention has become a reportable cause in itself, a new label for a new world. And, just as the travellers on the light rail in San Francisco were oblivious to the threat in their midst, police are finding that witnesses to crimes are becoming less and less useful to their investigations, because they simply didn't see anything.

It's not just traffic-related acts that are dangerous. Women are assaulted "out of nowhere", while jogging with headphones on. Fans turn to take selfies as a race passes by, unaware they are stepping into the path of the fast-moving competitors. We're losing our sense of space and our place in it, because attention is unable to reach out and find the edges for you.

While these situations are concerning, it's equally sad to see what people are missing in everyday life. Friends sit together in restaurants, cafes and bars but, in truth, they are miles apart. Once one person succumbs to the urge to look down, the rest fall like dominoes. Before long, a group of chatting friends fall silent as each are transported to their own virtual worlds. The one who stays present watches with a wry smile, waiting patiently until one of them re-emerges. She knows the battle is unwinnable.

The morning walk used to be a parade of passing "good mornings", but earphones may as well be blindfolds. A throng of people at a rock concert is now a sea of backlit smartphone faces. A live performance used to attract applause, but now it's muted. Hands are busy with a device, trying to capture the moment. At school concerts, kids no longer see the faces of their proud parents; instead it's the back of the device, as they

– O N E   M O M E N T   P L E A S E –

snap a moment to share, rather than sharing the moment as it happens. During intermission at a live play, people stay in their seats to check status updates, rather than mingling and sharing their thoughts about the performance. A blanket of smartphones covers social gatherings like a blanket of fog, just as disconnecting and disorienting.

Life experienced through a lens will never match life experienced through a sense. Memories are missed when your attention is missing. If your senses don't experience it, your brain cannot file it away for future reference. Taking photos to remember a place or an experience, will only help if you have first spent a moment really seeing it and experiencing it. Then later the photo can ignite the memory that your attention laid down. But you cannot achieve the same result the other way around.

'Here, stand together and I'll grab a photo.' The kids had just had their faces painted at the local school fair and finally found Dad, standing by his car flicking through his work emails. They smiled and huddled on demand, then gushed with stories about the fairy who painted them, and the other kids they had met. But his head was down and his grunts were perfunctory. 'I'm just uploading this, so Nanna and Gramps can see you.'

Back at home the pattern was the same. 'Daddy, one moment please!' she begged from across the room. But he was so absorbed in his mobile device that he didn't even hear her. She opted to perform her concert for the soft toys lined up in front of her. She looked like any other happy six-year-old, until you listened to her chatter. 'Teddy, turn around and look at me.'

Missing things, whether dangerous, unexpected, beautiful or curious, shuts you off from life. It's one of the factors that most affects your experience of the world, and often other people's too.

Sure, you're always going to miss something, because attention never did, and never will, notice it all. It's not meant to. But it is the only thing that will help you choose which experiences become part of your life.

MISSING YOURSELF > 'What's up with Peter?' she asked her colleague, genuinely concerned. Every time she saw the executive lately he looked unwell, tired, even dishevelled. And apparently, she wasn't the only one who noticed. Once an inspirational and charismatic leader, his team members were starting to complain about how hard it was to talk to him now. The next day, as she sat outside eating lunch in the warm spring sunshine, she saw him dart past. His shoulders were raised, tense around his ears, as he buried his nose in his mobile phone. She watched as he went from the office door to the local food outlet, waited for his order, and made his way straight back inside. He did not lift his head once, not even to acknowledge the person he nearly ran into, or the gutter that he tripped over. He certainly would not have noticed the beautiful weather or his colleagues sitting nearby.

The effect of having your attention pulled, stretched, split and scattered is stressful; it's also guaranteed to lower your performance. Without a healthy dose of control over what grabs your attention, it is easy for the feverish grip of "got to do it now" syndrome to take hold. It drives you toward multi-tasking, that alluring solution for getting more done. But by now you probably know that's an illusion. Some tasks are compatible enough to be managed by the synchrony of your brain in full flight, but so many are not. You're more likely to take 1.5 times longer doing things this way,[15] as you rip your attention from one finely-tuned set of neural networks to another. It's like leaving frayed ends when you hastily tear a piece of string—that is what you are doing when the thread of connection that your attention had been trying to attach for you is rudely ripped asunder. No wonder it's hard to remember where you left off, when you try to find your way back.

The "do more with less" revolution has undervalued the precious moments of idle time. Whether it's a queue in the post office, a lunch break at a training program, or waiting for a friend to join you for coffee, a break in proceedings is like a red rag to a bull. The device comes out to fill this seemingly useless moment with seemingly useful activity. Idle time has somehow earned itself a bad name, a label for laziness or sloth. But "idle" also means "at rest", and this is something that attention needs more than you may realise.

In the beautiful dance of the mind that starts with stimulating the senses and ends with taking action, we did not appreciate the silent steps of reflection, contemplation, and feeling that gave the dance meaning. During these steps, attention dives deep inside and weaves its magic with invisible threads that connect ideas with possibilities, experiences with meaning, and dreams with resolve. It's in the gaps between attentive tasks, when the mind is released from the tight grip of immediate matters that unexpected solutions, eureka moments, sudden realisations, and moments of clear insight can emerge. Without these moments, it is difficult to find the storyline of your own life. A quiet moment looking out the window on the bus may allow an answer to a problem you had been trying to solve for days to arise. A moment with your head lifted in a bank queue might lead to a conversation with your future spouse. A walk through the park on your way home can offer a perfect moment of clarity about a major change you've been avoiding.

We've shut the door to a large part of our mental experience, and we have evicted a valued tenant, our own steady source of wisdom, patience and insight. That tenant used to sit quietly on the porch, always ready to enter into a deep and reflective conversation. It was a place where confusion and quandary could sit safely until clarity returned, where challenges could rattle around open rooms and find solutions hidden in secret corners, where disappointment could be nursed until the pain passed, where passion could design a roadmap to purpose, and where mourning could learn to remember the good times. It was the place from which life could be observed.

In our ignorance, we swamped these rich moments with more noise, mistakenly assuming they were empty and wasted. Feeding attention an endless list of to-dos, carrying around a device that attention finds hard to resist, and training your attention to remain on high alert, means that it rarely rests.

A brain in a state of forced focus operates very differently to a brain set free. It's the difference between listening to one instrument or a whole orchestra. In a busy mind, attention jumps randomly from instrument to instrument, creating a cacophony of noise that holds little pleasure and delivers little reward. It's only when the busyness subsides, that attention opens widely enough to allow the rest of the orchestra to join in. It's the synchrony of many parts working in harmony that creates the magic.

SWITCHING OFF > It may be a saving grace that the life span of technology gets shorter and shorter, or maybe it's just our attention spans! But just as you get wise to the muggers' strategies, they change the game. Technology is a rapidly-evolving trickster and, when you lock the door to one con artist, the next climbs through the window and offers you an irresistible treat. Millions emigrate from social media platforms, getting out when they see through the deception that poses as connection, or wisdom, or a short-cut to success. Unfortunately they often migrate straight to the next big thing, replacing the freed-up space with a new attention trap.

Life—or what passes for it—flows constantly through these mobile devices. Emails, SMS, phone calls, alerts and updates come unbidden and, unless you take steps to protect yourself, each buzz or ding is a pickpocket slipping its hand in and escaping with a piece of attention. Every time it gets away with it, there's less left to nurture the rest of life.

There are signs suggesting that we're getting smart about how to weather the intensifying storm. 'I can't wait to tell you about my favourite app!' my friend exclaimed. 'You're going to love it. It detects all of your subscriptions and downloads them to one place, so you can unsubscribe from everything.' It's not unusual to receive an auto-response when you send someone an email that reads: *I only check my email at 10am and 3pm each day and will respond to your matter at these times.* People speak with pride about introducing device-free time into their life. Many people have successfully gone from inviting this mugger to join their family, to asking it to wait at the front gate until they're ready to come out.

But it will be hard to escape this chameleon, and to be honest, escape is not the answer. It will forever be part of your world, and it can be an incredibly powerful and useful part. The key is to find a way for your attention to live in harmony with it, not be overtaken by it.

CONFESSIONS OF A MUGGER VICTIM > Seven years was too long to feel disconnected from his wife and daughter. The rush he felt in his high-flying job paled by comparison to the rare moments of pure connection with his family. So one day he stopped. He didn't walk away and leave it all behind. He used to think that was the only answer, but it was not something he was prepared to do. He genuinely loved the business. But there was one thing he had never tried, and it had taken him a long time to realise it might actually work. Passing through his office door to head home that day became the line in the sand. Until he passed back through it next morning, work was finished. It was a mindset, but it triggered a whole series of actions he had not seriously tried before. He didn't ignore phone calls, but he didn't make them. He didn't check emails and he didn't finish any work left undone at the time he went home for the night. It could wait.

By the time he pulled into his garage, he had switched off from work by enjoying the passing landscape of his city. Even being stuck in traffic offered an opportunity for interesting observations that he would never have made previously. He would have been on the phone, wrapping up any loose ends he could find to fill the space!

As he entered his home, his mind was clear—a feeling so different to most other nights, when he felt like the constant busyness had accompanied him home like a rain cloud overhead. His ritual of half listening to his wife and children, while he was scrolling through messages, was replaced with just listening, empty handed and clear eyed. He knew it would make a difference, but the difference was astounding. Having gathered up the fragments of his attention so they were all home with him, he saw and heard new things about these people he had been taking for granted for much too long. He had conversations he could not have predicted, laughed along with jokes he had been missing, and was rewarded by a light in his children's eyes he had never noticed before.

As the night progressed, he realised that he had been living as if alone for so long, isolated from those he loved by his habits but, more importantly, by that mindset which made the grasping attention muggers more important than anyone else. He was determined to keep them in their place now: tools to enhance his performance, but tools only.

When he arrived at work next morning there was no crisis, no sting in the tail. His work was not impacted negatively at all. In fact, it was quite the opposite. The experiment at home had revealed that he was missing a lot right in front of him. So he wondered what else might emerge, if he applied the same principles at work. He went to meetings without his mobile phone and, because he was no longer tempted to check it while waiting for others to arrive, he greeted them instead. Now looking up, he became more aware of how people were feeling and what was on their mind. He saw things that he had been missing, adding vital depth to his decision-making.

He enjoyed lunch without his mobile phone as his companion. He felt more switched on in the afternoon. Eventually, he decided he would only check emails and messages at designated times, and the results were surprising. Ideas flowed more smoothly, connections with customers and colleagues improved, and the performance levels of his team climbed. It was all summed up by one employee in the staff survey: *He makes us feel like we are important and that makes us want to do better.*

5 Attention Thieves

IT'S ALL ABOUT ME > 'I know this is the busiest time of the day for you,' he began. 'You're not wrong!' she thought, cradling her six-week-old baby. 'But it's good for me, because I'm in the car driving home,' he continued. She struggled to listen with her baby in one arm, the phone under her chin, and the other hand making futile efforts to prepare dinner for her increasingly fractious toddler. He was a previous client and, for a moment, she inflated the call's importance. He continued on without drawing breath for twenty minutes, then abruptly blurted out, 'I've arrived at my destination. Gotta go now.' As the phone went clunk, she was left hanging on the other end feeling . . . robbed. This is the only way to describe it when your precious attention is stolen, not just from you, but from those you hold dear.

We have all been the victim of an attention thief, a person who, with total disregard for what you might be doing, elevates the priority of their own desire to share, their own need for action, curiosity, annoyance or excitement, or simply their desperation to fill their own empty void. They swoop in to seize one of your irreplaceable moments, then leave you dazed, wandering in circles, trying to find your way back to where you were before their intrusion. This is no small crime, because it can take up to twenty-five minutes to return to your original task after an interruption.[17] So, hours of precious attention can easily be lost to attention thieves throughout the day.

Our world turns on the exchange of attention, the only truly global commodity. Every person on this planet has a private stash, and you carry it with you every day. You spend it constantly, and there's always someone or something trying to steal some when you're not looking. But before you point the finger, admit it: you're guilty too. Thieving from others is generally unintentional and unconscious. In fact, it is usually with the very best of intent that we pick up the phone or lean over with the words, 'I just have to tell you this!' We are driven by our own agenda, and rarely notice that it does not always align with the agendas of others.

Rather than waiting for the right moment, we intrude whenever we feel the urge. And you are most likely to gatecrash the people closest to you. They are the ones whose attention we most crave, the ones we know will entertain the intrusion, or maybe just the ones we feel least guilty thieving from. 'Mum! Where are my socks?' Mr Seven always struggled to complete the morning's routine without an inane cry for attention. In fact, he was an accomplished thief, and Mum fell for it every time.

The truth is, it might just be impossible to avoid this crime, for we are all born master thieves. A baby's cry will grab your attention; impossible to ignore, even if it's not your baby. And when it **is** your baby, it's a siren call that will cut through sleep, background noise and distraction. Your brain floods with hormones that force you to give your most precious gift and, now connected, you can fulfil your child's deepest needs. A human child depends on the caring attention of adults for longer than any other animal on this planet. Our very survival rests on our talent for attracting attention. Crying is only the first in a series of raids you will commit on other people's attention throughout your life. You'll giggle and gurgle, toddle and chatter, pout and sigh, hover and nag, throw a tantrum and use the silent treatment.

Some of these tricks continue on into adulthood. Whether you engage in a life of crime or become a reformed offender can depend in large part on how much you have had to fight to gain this precious resource. As attention becomes scarcer, harder to attract, and too often withheld, we breed a generation of attention thieves. And these thieves go on in life to pay the crime forward.

'It's verging on bullying. One day she's nice, then the next day she'll be starting cruel rumours. The final straw was when she sent a group SMS to all the kids, declaring that another girl was mean because she had stopped talking to her. Over the next few days she continued sending messages, even though most of the kids were ignoring them. Eventually the messages changed tone, and she was pleading for the other girl to reconnect with her. When you know this girl, you realise she cannot stand it if she's not the centre of attention.' Neediness doesn't emerge from thin air. This form of attention thievery is the legacy of attention starvation. When this life-giving force is withheld, particularly at crucial stages in early life, the urge to shoplift attention can become insatiable. It is anxiety that drives the thieving behaviour but, even when the gift is received, the fear of losing it again maintains a sad cycle that devalues the currency of care.

THE EARLY YEARS OF ATTENTION > It is the stuff of our mysterious and amazing physical world that children are most drawn to, and what they most need in this journey to map their world: human interaction, the great outdoors, and the sounds, movement and feel of real life. Attention compels them to touch everything, put things in their mouths, watch intently for long periods, and ask questions endlessly. They must return again and again to the same places, the same experiences and the same ideas, until each takes on a life of its own within their minds. They must mimic, play, wrestle, copy and compete. All is new and nothing is yet tainted by opinion, judgment or assumption. Those things come later.

During the early years, there is no substitute for the generous and steady attention of an adult. You are their attention guide during these years, and there are three crucial roles you must play, if they are to realise their potential. The first is to create a secure environment, so that their attention is not forced to divert to watch for danger. This is something their attention will turn itself to later in life. But if they become too alert to threat in these early years, anxiety takes the place that should be filled by enthusiasm, and their learning is hindered.

Your second role as a young child's attention guide is to draw their already powerful gift further out into the world. They will notice so much more than you realise but, with just a few questions, a bit of encouragement and a lot of patience, you can help them design a map with longer roads and more pathways. Why just nod when they point up and say "bird"? Why not draw their attention to the birds that sit in the tree to the right, and behind, helping them to map a bigger picture with greater depth and meaning? All you need to do is take their lead, then help them go as deep as they are ready to go. The key is not to distract or divert them, but to extend and encourage them.

Your third role is to teach them how to harness this formidable force, so it grows into a clear, flowing stream, connecting them to the most important things in life. It means raising them to understand that their attention is precious. It means making sure they taste the deeply rewarding satisfaction of impulse control, and not just the short hit of the quick fix. It means creating the space for them to dive deeply into their own sense of self, then plumb those depths for their strengths, passions and purpose. In doing this, your actions speak louder than words, because mirroring and mimicking are natural learning methods in the early years.

'I'm bored.' She always dreaded the school holidays. No matter how well planned she was, it seemed impossible to keep them entertained. 'Don't tell me you've already finished your paintings? I'll get the dress-up box out, but can I just finish my coffee?' They wandered off but she couldn't relax now, so she pushed aside her study papers and went to the cupboard to pull the next game out. 'If I don't have something to put in front of them, they'll just fight. It's the only way to keep them occupied and leave me some space to keep studying.'

Children have X-ray eyes, sniffing out the difference between your words and your actions. If you abuse your own attention, exposing it to junk thoughts and fast moves, they will not learn to value this precious gift. Like you, they will treat it as disposal income, rather than a lifelong investment. If they see you fall for the attention muggers' tricks, they will similarly forego the patient long game for the thrill of a few early goals, draining their impulse control with every worthless indulgence. If you keep them occupied on the surface of life, you are holding them back from a place they may never learn exists: their own deeper self.

Boredom is one of the greatest experiences you can give a child. It must be experienced during these early years, if they are to have any chance of surviving in a world where attention is constantly under assault. Until faced with this empty space, until they can feel its full width and breadth, they will never learn to let their attention uncoil to its full potential. Like a stabled horse, a child whose mind is constantly entertained develops a short and restless attention span, always reined back in too soon. Fed with answers, protected from failure, and steered through possibilities, how can such children learn the deep satisfaction of breaking through, the awe of discovery, and the pleasure of finding their own connections with life? They grow as they have been nurtured. The pathways they will need later to be comfortable in their own skins and fulfil lives of real purpose must be laid down early.

ATTENTION BABYSITTERS > The needs of a child's attention are not the same as for an adult. In a rush to fill every moment, or through misinterpreting their real need, or maybe out of pure exhaustion, you can inadvertently disrupt the glorious flow of their attention, leaving it unable to find its own rhythm and reason. It's fertile training ground for the next generation of attention thieves who can't sit still, crave constant stimulation, and expect it all to come to them. This fragile gift can be too easily damaged by overexposure, and it can be contaminated by your own anxieties.

'Don't go down that slope. It's too dangerous!' The words were out of her mouth before she could retract them, and she saw the fear rise up in her six-year-old daughter, as she turned back to face her. She was grateful when her husband intervened with, 'Don't worry, Mummy just skied down there and had a bit of a fall, because she forgot to lean forward. But you'll be right, you're great at that.' And with those words the confidence flooded back, and she pushed off and skied away. Mummy promptly booked herself into a class with an experienced ski instructor. 'I realised I needed to get out of the way and not burden her with my own fears. She was more than capable, but I could so easily have convinced her that she was not.'

Nurturing attention is crucial for giving children the very best start in life; but when you're busy, distracted or tired, their endless curiosity can feel like a constant barrage on your own attention. Now, more than ever, it seems children are surrounded by "attention babysitters": a veil of dangling toys hanging from their stroller, a device thrust in their hands at a cafe, a series of organised activities planned with military precision to get them through school holidays. But once you expose them to things that block or distract their attention, you hinder their journey of discovery.

'Have you seen how many babies in prams have a book or a tablet stuck in front of their face? It's not just in coffee shops or bank queues, where I could see that people might be trying to distract them for a while, but I see it while they're being pushed in a stroller through the park.' Children become the unintended victims in this war gone wrong. As the battle for attention rages all around, they hear things they do not need to know, see things that create nightmares, become swamped by noise, and get hurried along and tricked into switching their attention off.

'Dad, you were so right. Those DVD players in the car are a disaster!' Despite her father's best efforts to convince her not to get them, this young mum had gone with the advice of her various friends, who insisted she would be very pleased to have them. 'They were great for the five-hour drive to our camping trip at Easter, but I knew I should have taken them out when we got back. So they've been jumping in the car after school and putting the headphones straight on, and I still didn't do anything. But last night was the clincher. When I asked Jess what she did at school she just said, "Mummy, don't talk to me." She was so blunt it shocked me, and I realised how much damage this was doing. In the short trip from school to home, I may as well have wiped clean everything she had learnt that day. You'll be glad to know I've taken them out and packed them away until the next long trip.'

A group of eight-year-olds, when asked to describe grandparents, might just have hit on the very best advice for raising kids with healthy attention habits:

- They don't say, 'Hurry up.'

- When they take us for walks, they slow down past things like pretty leaves and caterpillars.

- When they read to us, they don't skip. They don't mind if we ask for the same story over again.

- Everybody should have a grandmother, especially if you don't have television, because they are the only grown-ups who like to spend time with us.[18]

Children cannot get on with the urgent work of learning and growing, unless they are provided with everything that flows through your own healthy stream of attention: security, encouragement, direction and love. But you are only a guide in nature's flow.

INTERRUPTION INVASION > Sure, there have always been attention thieves, triggered by whatever personal experience has caused them to reach out more than most. But skip back just one generation, and it was more likely that you could indulge in the pleasure of focusing on what you were doing, without being interrupted by a phone call about a friend's dog or a text about the latest dating escapade. You simply didn't phone people on landlines about such random stuff. Protected by the fixedness of a phone's location and the limited chance of actually catching someone at the other end, more thought was put into the import-ance of the information and whether it could wait until later.

Although it may not have been a conscious act, there was more respect for other people's attention. Many homes had rules about times during which it was acceptable to make and receive calls: never during dinner time, never after 9pm, and a call before school or work in the morning would most likely have been something urgent and unexpected. People saved the latest news for face-to-face interactions, often over a meal. That was a special time of connection. But maybe the reason everyone is "instagramming" their meal, updating their status, and grabbing selfies with the waiters is because they've got nothing left to talk about, after a week of constant but mindless sharing!

Once you understand the precious nature of attention, and how fragile and limited it really is, it won't take long before you become sensitive to both committing the act of attention theft and having it committed on you. You'll see it everywhere, every day. You'll notice when your head is turned by an unwelcome intrusion, you'll recognise when you've been sucked down a vortex of intrigue, and you'll catch yourself in the act of "break and enter" violations you didn't realise you committed.

"Excuse me?" or "Can you talk?" or "Are you in the middle of anything?" These are the questions a polite attention thief uses to quietly break the lock. Once the words are out, the deed is already done, but it does not mean you will leave with the stolen goods. While few people overtly reject you when you're being an attention thief, you are probably just one of many things grasping for their limited and fragile resource. So you may not be able to successfully steal as much as you were seeking. If you often receive a, 'That's nice, dear,' or a delayed, 'What was that you asked me?' then your intended victim probably has little attention for you to steal. Rather than ramping up your attacks, or brooding because you think they are an attention withholder, perhaps the best response is to deposit a good dose of attention into the situation, get back in tune with others, and work in harmony with the flow of attention.

'Am I totally missing something?! Why are mothers struggling so much these days? Is it really that hard?' It was a Monday afternoon and my carefree, single (and child-free) friend had called searching for answers. A successful businesswoman, she had just hung up from a frustrating call with a frazzled mother. To complete her client's loan application, she needed just a few more answers. After failing to catch her at home, she'd tracked her down on her mobile phone, hands-free and with three noisy kids in the background. The call had finished abruptly with her client saying that she would not be able to deal with it until her kids were in bed.

This wasn't the first encounter my friend had experienced with overwhelmed mums lately. 'Really, are mothers just too soft these days? I never remember my mum getting frazzled or not being able to answer a question because there were kids in the car!' 'You're 100 percent right,' I said. 'When our mums were raising young kids, there was no way to contact them after they left the house.' The mobile device is often the weapon of choice for the attention thief, because attention finds technology incredibly alluring. My friend went silent and I could sense that the gravity of this realisation had hit home. 'I wonder if I should have left my call until tonight?' my friend reflected. 'It wasn't actually that urgent; I just wanted to get the paperwork off my desk.'

THE BUSINESS OF ATTENTION THEFT > Attention thieves pounce from unexpected sources, often those you thought you could trust. Media thrives on the fact that attention is much more alert to threat and danger, so it's no coincidence that the stories on the nightly news are predominantly about things that are going wrong in the world. There are undoubtedly just as many good and wonderful stories unfolding across the globe; but they know that the negatives will win you over faster and keep you coming back. We are wired to share stories that might teach us something but, if we're not careful, we become repeater stations for someone else's messages, inadvertently steering our friends and family members into the thief's ambush.

'I heard that people got sick after eating there.' Rumour and innuendo are powerful thieves, difficult to ignore. But so often you find later that you have wasted your precious attention on something that had little foundation; you realise you have been an accomplice in a form of collective attention theft that can ruin reputations, drive a business to the edge of destruction, or drive an individual to the brink of despair.

When you hold attention, you hold the key to the greatest prize of all. Those who recruit the greatest amount of attention win something much more important than just your money or your time. Attention is the gateway to thought, feeling, consideration, decision and action. Those who recruit the greatest amount of attention turn humanity to their agenda and, by doing so, they change the world.

Your attention is easily skewed by the faceless decision-makers who set the agenda for the daily paper and the nightly news. It is steered by "opinion-makers", who only want to hold your interest for as long as it takes to win a campaign or finish their chat show. Increasingly sophisticated theft rackets are masterminded to advertise products, win followers, promote ideas and motivate action. Websites, emails, newsletters, social media campaigns and ads are all screaming out for attention. At every turn, you run the risk that an attention thief will slip under your guard, extract part of your daily store, and escape before you realise what just happened.

Ever since famous salesman Zig Ziglar said, 'Sell the sizzle, not the steak,' advertising's main focus has been to mine attention. It's an industry that casts spells with bewitching words, such as "final days" and "last pair on sale", terms that have an uncanny way of triggering the fear of missing out. If you have an item in your cupboard that was bought while you were under the spell of an advertising attention thief, there's a fair chance you have never used it or worn it. Often the sight of these items triggers a visceral memory of the larceny committed on you, and you feel robbed all over again! Some salespeople have graduated from the school of fear to the school of reward. Rather than first making you feel vulnerable, then swooping while your control is weak, they aim instead to make you feel inspired, elated and engaged. And from this state, they do not overtly steal your attention, but convince you to give it willingly. It is still possible to later feel robbed by this approach. Wearing a certain watch or driving a certain car won't turn your life into a *James Bond* movie.

It is only when those things that you care most deeply about genuinely align with what someone else is offering that the connection is true. Then you will give your attention without any trickery or persuasion. Instead of being robbed, your precious resource is rewarded with the perfect trade.

The business world is full of the push and pull of attention thieves. And it's not just those wanting to sell you something. In every direction, more and more raids on attention are committed, as people struggle to be heard. Clients steal from their service providers, employees steal from their bosses, bureaucrats steal from the public, the public steal from officials, colleagues steal from each other, and the list goes on.

When the topic of attention in the workplace is raised, conversation inevitably turns to the open plan office. The loud co-worker six desks down seems to have the perfect pitch for catching your ear. And the girl you regret befriending now comes uninvited to sit opposite and unload her daily dose of frustration on you. But look deeper: attention is being endlessly stolen in subtle and seemingly justifiable ways. A new policy to protect employee privacy means there are now three layers of paperwork required to provide staff names to the external trainer who will spend the day with them. A satisfied manager, wanting to fast-track payment to a cherished service provider, can only do so if he prepares a full business case for the variation. A workshop to develop a business plan comes up with some great ideas, but the final version of the document just looks like last year's and the participants are disappointed. A rebranding of the internal communication materials means that there is a new process to become familiar with, but it makes no difference to business outcomes. Worse still are the cases of conflicting messages. A manager calls the team in to update them on the new company vision, but "off the record" tells them to just keep doing things the old way.

'It's unbelievable! Last year, fifteen million emails were sent by our company. And the crazy thing is only 5 percent of those went externally to our actual customers!' she exclaimed. She stopped to ponder what was behind the high volume and continued, tongue-in-cheek, 'People are emailing about everything these days, even the things that should really be handled in a face-to-face conversation. And even if they do talk first, they still follow up with an email, because they don't trust each other, so they want it in writing. And we're copying in anyone who might have a vague interest: the legal and HR departments so your butt is covered, the person who sits in front of you, because you are too lazy to get out of your seat, and your own superiors so you look good. Then everyone complains that they are so busy they need to recruit more staff!'

ROBBED OF THEIR PURPOSE > Sometimes it is businesses demanding more attention from us, and at other times we are the culprits, robbing their attention from the things that matter. This was the case when a group of overzealous Grade 1 parents lobbied their children's teacher for a daily email detailing the activities she had completed with the kids. These keen parents had experienced something quite common with five-year-olds: when you ask what they did today, they just don't reveal much. These parents wanted to be more involved, and thought that going direct to the teacher would arm them better.

But consider the impact of this one simple request. This is a teacher who is recognised for her amazing ability to connect with the kids and keep them enthusiastically engaged all day. This requires the generous gift of attention, and she is naturally adept at giving it where it is most needed. To ask her to give even a small portion to one more administrative task is to ask her to withhold just a little from the kids. Because, just like you and me, her attention bandwidth is limited and, just like you and me, this precious resource is already committed to a range of other demands. It's a vicious cycle, because we all pay a price for adding more without taking something away. An extra email in an already busy inbox just raises stress levels and sucks attention away from elsewhere.

Similar demands are being made on doctors, nurses, police, project managers, builders and plumbers; in fact, people in all types of businesses are expected to give their attention to layers of additional activity and administration. At the time these expectations are created, there's always a reason why someone believes this issue deserves attention. But consideration is rarely given to the reality that attention must be stolen from elsewhere to add this new item. Most of us have packed our attention bandwidth until it is completely full. So the answer rests not in asking, 'What do we need more of?' but in asking, 'What matters most?'

Because we can't do it all, we won't notice it all, and we don't need it all. And when we stop expecting it all, we will finally have the motivation to stop stealing other people's attention. Only then will the balance return, and then they will be able to give it willingly.

CARE, NOT ISOLATION > 'But I need to debrief with my besties! It's good for me to have a whinge and get it out of my system.' But often we don't check the impact it has on the other person. Maybe the real reason for the saying "a problem shared is a problem halved" is that you pass half of it on to someone else to carry!

'I avoid phone calls from her now. Last week, when I had half an hour spare before my next appointment, she called. I was sorry I picked up the phone, because she was in a foul mood, going over and over an issue that we had also gone over and over last week and the week before. And the thing is, I felt a great deal of compassion for her, but she did not want to deal with it, she just wanted to go over and over it. I don't think it mattered to her who was on the other end of the phone. She just needed to vent, again. When I hung up the phone, I was physically exhausted. My previous light mood was replaced with one that was dark and heavy. The quantity and quality of my attention for the next person, who desperately needed it, was severely depleted. My friend would not have given it another thought. In fact she was back doing business with the same person she was whinging about the very next week!'

It's probably not possible to exist without being an occasional thief. There are times when we all interrupt each other, and in small doses that's okay. But as you develop a growing appreciation for the precious and fragile nature of attention, you are more likely to see how you could maybe not send that email, contact your friend at a better time than right now, and try for just a little longer to find that missing sock before asking for help. A small choice, the hesitation that comes from healthy impulse control, can make a big difference.

CONFESSIONS OF AN ATTENTION THIEF > It didn't take her long to recognise she was an attention thief. 'I've been doing it in so many ways. My kids, my friends and my staff members have all been my victims. I use the tablet devices to keep my kids quiet at a cafe. I message my friends about things that happen to me throughout the day. I send my staff members emails whenever something comes to mind, even though they sit just a few steps away from me. And I download the dramas of the day to my husband each night.'

She realised that her hectic days were largely of her own making. By thieving from others, she was also abusing her own attention. So she decided to give up the crime of attention theft and see what happened. She implemented a new rule for screen-free meal times: no games, devices or television. After a few days of whining, some interesting new family traditions emerged. Breakfast was calmer and everyone seemed more organised. Dinner became a fascinating parade of stories, ideas, debates and laughter. And while a visit to a cafe offered less adult time, the kids learnt so much more by watching the world around them.

Every time she was about to send a message to one of her friends, she checked herself. Did this message merit the bit of valuable attention that it would cost her friend? Did it need to be done now, or could it wait until the next time they were together? Over time, she realised most of these fleeting thoughts and comments were so meaningless that she couldn't even remember them later. It was often idle gossip, frivolous commentary, or unnecessary judgment. The conversations she did have with her friends became more fulfilling. She started to listen more, giving them the gift of attention rather than taking it away, and it was making her feel happier.

At work, she started writing lists whenever something came to mind, then had a short chat with each staff member to talk through the issues only once or twice a day. She realised that they had been losing their train of thought every time she hit them with a random email. Now they were able to stay focused on a task, without the intrusion of her "attention missiles". Eventually the whole team agreed they wanted to ban emails to each other altogether, and talk face–to–face when something needed attention.

'And without dramas ruling my day, conversations at home with my husband have been transformed. We share so many more interesting things that happen in our day, and we've found a depth that we had overlooked for far too long.'

6 Space Invaders

LITTLE VOICES > Jill Bolte Taylor is a neuroanatomist, someone whose work is dedicated to understanding the brain. In an unexpected twist, Jill had a front row seat to the mysterious nature of attention, when she experienced a stroke. She was unable to walk and talk, but her most revealing experience was her inability to talk to herself. There was no internal chatter, nothing to which attention could attach itself. She was unable to connect to memories of the past or dreams of the future and, in the absence of this rich flow of internal dialogue, she also lost all sense of self. There was literally nothing; everything that had ever defined her was gone. You might expect that Jill's reaction in the face of such a disarming experience would be fear or panic, but instead it was one that sounds a lot more like relief: 'Those little voices were delightfully silent.'[19] When you escape the muggers, the thieves and the daily grind, do you find peace and quiet, or do your own noisy thoughts invade this space? Thoughts tumble over each other in a race for your attention, playing tricks to push themselves forward for a piece of the action. It has been postulated that anywhere from 12,000 to 70,000 thoughts pass through the mind each day. Authorities might rush to ban the use of mobile phones while driving, but little consideration is given to an equally dangerous misdemeanour: driving while under the influence of worries, re-runs or the endless to-do list. Your own thoughts can be as distracting as a mobile device. And they both lead to the same result: a mind not on the job.

Thankfully, you won't notice many of your thoughts; but there is no doubt that the busy mind syndrome is on the rise, and it's no surprise. When your attention is constantly battered by new information, change and choice, it sets your mind off on a journey to understand, consider and decide. When your attention has become accustomed to flicking between devices, even when you are faced with nothing to do, the habit of your mind continues.

Thoughts are the powerhouse of your existence, translating knowledge into meaning, linking experiences to emotion, and turning ideas into action. If the chatter seems constant, it is— with a thought passing through your mind, on average, every six to ten seconds. Some quietly do their job in the background without any fanfare, some pass by without leaving a mark, but others gather you up on their exciting journey and take you far, far away . . .

THE PERILS OF A WANDERING MIND > Your attention will wander most during familiar activities like grooming, commuting and housework.[2] In these and many other habitual pursuits— like cooking, eating and, unfortunately, working—it is common for attention to wander 50–60 percent of the time. Your body knows the moves so well that it can operate in a state akin to autopilot. The well-worn pathways in your brain will guide your actions with the minimum of energy expenditure, and almost no attention, leaving it at a dangerous loose end.

If you find yourself pulling into your garage with no memory of the trip home, finishing your dinner but not really tasting it, picking up the shampoo bottle then wondering if you've already washed your hair, or sending an email then panicking about whether you accidentally sent it to the person you were complaining about, then you've been on autopilot. It's a normal mechanism that helps you get through routine and habit with the minimum of effort. But if you've only had 40 percent of your attention switched onto the task, what's happened to the rest? When it's left at a loose end, attention will not slumber; it will wander.

It makes the job of attention thieves and muggers that much easier, but even they will struggle to compete with the block-buster movies in your own mind.

Attention loves to play indoors, spoilt for choice in the rich store of your memories, your fears and your imaginings. Thought moves at lightning speed, and a whole movie can play through your mind in the moment it takes to draw breath. But you can get lost for much longer, as the circling thoughts draw you more deeply into what might have been, or what could be. When attention is captivated by the stories in your mind, sound reaches the ears but is not heard, and light reaches the eyes but is not seen. Attention cannot be in two places at once, and this is why mistakes are made, experiences are missed, and loved ones feel neglected.

THE MOVIES IN YOUR MIND > Attention breathes life into your thoughts. When it is given to the ideas you want to grow, the vision you want to create, and the experiences you want to celebrate, attention reveals a glorious pathway through life and fills you with the vitality to act. But when it is given repeatedly to the experiences you regret, doubts of your own ability or fears that may never come to pass, the path is blocked, you feel held back and your energy is drained.

Some of the movies in your mind can seem more real than life itself. As the actors take their places on set, these stories ambush your attention and draw you inexorably to the world within. Thoughts feed on your attention, becoming more animated and vibrant with each passing moment. If you're not careful, they will take on the shape of your deepest fears, often telling a tale more terrifying than life itself.

'I don't remember the journey home at all. I don't even know if I said goodbye to my team members.' It had been a big day and the pressure was mounting in her project at work. The boss was concerned that things weren't moving fast enough. She knew the only way she could speed it up was to get the other team to move things along, but they didn't like someone from "outside" telling them what to do. 'I was so worried about how I would raise it with them. No matter which way I played it out, it all ended badly. I had visions of them being really rude, walking out on me, or complaining about me to the boss. By the time I got home, I was convinced I was going to lose my job, we'd have to sell our new house, and I was almost crying when I walked through the front door.'

So you rehash the problems from the day on your drive home, then can't remember how you got there. You wonder what you're missing on TV while you're at a business dinner, and promptly forget everyone's names. You mentally rehearse the tough discussion you need to have with your boss while eating breakfast, and spill your coffee on your suit. You tell yourself over and over again that you'll never get the promotion while you're filling the dishwasher, then find the dishes still dirty in the morning, because you neglected to turn it on.

A wandering mind is an unhappy mind, and it's not just because your attention is most easily captured by negatives. It's because you are missing out on life as it unfolds around you.

'Don't you just love Paris in the springtime? The light is so soft. It looks like a watercolour painting. Honey, don't you agree?' 'Huh?' he replied, lifting his head and looking at her like she was a stranger he had bumped into on the street. When attention wanders, something physical is lost. Snatched away and carried off by whatever whim or worry intrudes, life's animating force pulls out, leaving the body with only the bare necessities. The sparkle in the eyes fades and the head lowers, the body's way of limiting the amount of distraction coming through the sense of sight. The other senses are similarly deactivated, but the most significant sign is the loss of vigour and vitality in the body. There's a sag in the posture, no spring in the step, and a blankness of face. You become almost robotic, denied of the vibrancy that attention imbues, and denying others of a connection with you.

When attention is lost to the things that drain you of joy, meaning, inspiration and encouragement, you become emotionally, spiritually and physically depleted. You can be sure that if you end a day exhausted, but have undertaken little physical activity, it is the fruitless overworking of your attention that has wrung you out. The brain is the organ in the body that uses the most energy, and when all it's doing is chewing on circling thoughts, there is no nourishment for body or soul.

And if none of that motivates you to pay attention, hear this: 'Did you notice the guys in this group got better looking when they practised paying attention?' she whispered during a break in the training program. Filled with this animating force, there is no doubt she was right!

NOT A HAPPY ENDING > The first thing to be discarded in an overwhelmed life is "me time", the space to nurture your health, your spirit and your path through life. But ironically, the most destructive inner thoughts that steal your attention away are "me thoughts". Your own picture of the world acts as a prism through which all things are experienced. And it is your opinions, your preferences, your judgments, your likes, your dislikes and your own assumptions that you hear most loudly in your mind. Attention does not just deliver you the facts of a situation. It likes to spice things up by going inside and pulling up your reaction. And once it senses a big one, it will dwell there. This is why you'll find yourself re-running a situation that caused you pain, or worrying about the work you've been putting off. It's why a slight by a colleague is the one thing you rant on about at home, when someone asks about your day.

Heart-rending dramas are more compelling than heart-warming ones, and the most gripping movies in your mind are not those with happy endings, but those where danger lurks at every turn. So, if you find it easier to dwell on your worries, re-run the most difficult parts of your day, or picture the worst-case scenario, it's only natural. And there is an explanation.

Your brain processes negative and positive information differently, with the negative being most quickly registered, stored and recalled. Fears, inequities, heartbreak, pain and doubt will grab your attention more quickly, and hold onto it for longer. It's a survival advantage to be more alert to danger, than to the happy or harmless events of the day. But your attention doesn't know the difference between a real and present danger, and one conjured up by your imagination. So it is too often captured by dangers that may never come to pass, leaving little to nourish what is here now.

Your brain wants to be your best friend, but it won't distinguish between what's good for you and what's bad for you. It simply perfects what you practise, and leaves you to live with the consequences. If you dwell on everything still lingering on your to-do list, you are guaranteed to feel busy. If you re-run a bad experience, you will feel the pain all over again. And if you don't direct your attention towards new ways of thinking, you will get stuck in the rut of familiarity. Or perhaps you'll catch someone else's mood and start complaining without any good reason to do so. What you focus on grows. Thoughts will always flow, but it is only attention that can make them grow. The precious gift of attention nourishes a thought, like a rain shower nourishes a budding plant. And just as weeds grow more easily in an untended garden, so too do negative thoughts grow more easily in an untended mind. They invade quickly, and it doesn't take them long to spread through the landscape of your mind, until all else is eclipsed.

ATTENTION GRABBERS > There are seven attention grabbers that show up again and again, when people reveal which thoughts take them furthest away from the life they want to live. Fears will paralyse you; negative "self talk" will zap your confidence; ruts will keep you living the same life you did yesterday; re-runs will keep you stuck in the past; to-dos will keep you in an endless cycle of busyness; viruses will make other people's problems yours to share; and what-ifs will create anxiety about the future.

1. What-Ifs

'If she misses out on the school we really want, we'll be devastated. I just don't want her to go to a school where she might fall in with a bad group, particularly if she doesn't turn out to be very academic. What if she turns to drugs to cope?' In a matter of moments, this mother had lived through the horror of watching her sweet two-year-old daughter become a crack addict, and the stress showed. Her body was tense and her eyes were haunted. It was only the loud crash of a glass falling from a nearby table that dragged her attention back out of the dark theatre of her mind and into the noisy, light-filled restaurant, where she sat surrounded by her friends.

Stress and anxiety are the constant companions of those who allow their attention to become lost in worries, what-ifs, judgements and fears. Feeding your mind stories that keep it on high alert and watchful for danger, leaves no room for your attention to cultivate the positives in life. Even at the best of times, your attention is a limited resource. But once your threat response switches on, attention becomes even more narrowed, targeting in on the source of threat and shutting out anything unrelated. Your body tenses in preparation to battle this threat, or run quickly from its claws. This wonderful mechanism, that saves your life in the face of sudden physical threat, is debilitating when it remains switched on for hours, days, or even years, trying to save you from something that hasn't even happened— and probably never will.

If you allow your attention to be grabbed by what-ifs, they will consume it. Fed a constant diet of negativity, your attention can only lead you down the path of avoidance, retreat, defence or defiance. In the grip of these attention grabbers, you will flinch in the face of an opportunity, regretting later the missed moment of choice, when you could have moved forward but instead pulled back.

'I've suffered from anxiety for as long as I can remember, but I think it really started after my divorce. I worried about the impact on my children and that I might never find a life partner again. Before long, I was worrying about everything: whether I'd lose my job, whether my kids would find friends at school, and it even extended to little things like whether the bus would arrive on time.'

What-ifs are stories about the future, but they can only ever be one possible version: a guess based on scant facts and lots of assumptions. Attention jumps through the pictures in your mind and cobbles together a scenario, but there are only certain situations in life where this is a productive exercise. 'We spent the day planning how we would make the changes we needed in our business. It helped us to see an opportunity we had been overlooking, and I was glad we took the time out with the team to do it. But there was one side effect I had not predicted. One of the team members seemed more distracted than normal over the following weeks, so I finally asked him what was wrong. It turns out he had assumed there wouldn't be a place for him in the company's new direction, and he had been worrying about his future. Instead of talking to me about it, he had just made some big assumptions. He told me that he had come in every day expecting to be told he was being let go. I couldn't believe how far from the truth his mind had taken him."

When it comes to what-ifs, there is one thing for sure: no matter what pictures your busy mind conjures up, real life will be different. In fact, it's been suggested that as many as 80 percent of your what-ifs never come true, but as long as you keep your attention stuck on this picture, it's hard to even see real life as it unfolds.

2. Fears

One of attention's most crucial roles is to alert you to danger. Fear is the emotion it recruits for this task. But it is not the slithering snake or deadly spider that will steal your attention away for lengthy periods. Most physical threats arise and pass quickly. But social and emotional threats rarely do.

The fear of failure, fear of losing control, fear of standing out, fear of missing out, and fear of facing the truth are five fears that we explored in our book, *Wired for Life*.[20] You'll find their origins in survival challenges faced by the earliest humans but, in our modern world, they keep your attention focused on surviving at the expense of thriving.

With the fear of failure, your attention becomes captured by potential risks. The likelihood of failure dominates your thinking, overshadowing any other possibilities. It feels like there is no option but to retreat from the opportunities presented to you. But it is the ultimate act of self-sabotage, because not taking a chance at something that will bring fulfilment is the true source of failure. And don't forget that some of the greatest moments of learning and growth emerge from failure, so to judge it as the enemy just shuts down one of the surest paths to success.

With the fear of losing control, you become convinced that the plan in your head is the one you must follow, even as life unfolds differently. Departing from the plan makes you feel out of control, so you seek to remove that discomfort by giving all your energy to shaping the world so it fits once more with your mind's picture. But this fear has lead you into a battle with life, a battle for control that you can never win. Extraordinary moments happen off-plan; life most often reveals itself when you let go.

With the fear of standing out, blending in and staying safe in the crowd seems sensible, even essential. "Belonging" is a desirable state, and the glaring scrutiny that comes with standing out increases the risk of rejection. The fear will make you hesitate to step up or speak out, but in truth, it is forcing you to bury your authentic and unique self. It can leave haunting regret that is only appeased when you finally find your voice.

With the fear of missing out, you slip into thinking you need to take every passing opportunity without even checking its true value. It triggers a scarcity mentality, which drives material accumulation, a competitive nature, or the anxiety of constant vigilance. When overcome by this fear, satisfaction is fleeting, and the joy of collaboration and sharing are overlooked. Much more can be achieved by an abundance mentality where opportunities are seen for their true value and taken for the right reasons.

In a sneaky twist, the fear of facing the truth underlies the victim mentality. Deflecting blame and responsibility starts off as a survival strategy, but becomes a deeply entrenched and highly addictive bad habit. Eventually you forget the truth, which is that you alone have the power to achieve your dreams. Acting as though someone else or something else has thwarted you is disempowering.

These fears become a powerful force when they receive your attention. What you focus on grows, so they will loom larger than they really are, if you animate them with attention's convincing force. Attention quickly develops a taste for danger, fear and anxiety. Thoughts that are heavily seasoned with risk, spicy with drama and sticky with emotion are particularly addictive. But they're unhealthy and they starve you of the vital nutrients that come from a life focused on purpose and lived in the present.

If you choose to view an idea, an opportunity, a response or a situation as a threat, you are the architect of your own fear. When the person next to you views the same thing as an opportunity, they are engaged and they act, while you retreat and hide. It shows you how deeply important the choice about where you give your attention can be on life's journey.

3. To-Dos

Studies of diaries indicate that perhaps we are not all as busy as we think we are.[21] But if you feel busy, it could be the internal chatter that makes you feel the burden of so many things left undone. If you recite your to-do list in your head, from the moment you wake until you close your eyes at night, you're circling your precious attention endlessly over rocky terrain. It's not going to return with sudden wonderful news that all is done, all is finished, and that well-deserved clear space is finally upon you. It will return with the same message as last time: your looming obligations remain. You will feel busy, you will feel overwhelmed, and the fear of not getting it all done will force your precious attention out once more to check the fences.

Attention can't find its way to clarity by pushing further into busyness. It will come to a grinding halt. But if you hit the pause button earlier and give it some space to regroup it can find the stepping stones that will take you through to the other side.

'I can't stop thinking about all the things I have to get done! There is so much to do that it paralyses me. I don't know where to start and I end up doing nothing—except stress!'

Stress is rarely caused by the activity that you are engaged in at the time. It arises from staring at the yawning gap between the things you **think** you should be doing and the things you have actually done. And when your attention is caught on the plan in your head of how life **should** unfold, and fixated on where you are trying to get, you miss the wonder in every moment.

4. Ruts

It may be surprising to hear that a large proportion of the thoughts you'll have today will be the same ones you had yesterday. You have been training your brain since the day you were born. When you practise something over and over again, your brain lays down pathways that become the ruts you follow in many daily activities. We are creatures of habit, because it's efficient for the brain to do things the same way as before, but it might not be effective for the next situation you face. When attention senses a useful rut to slip into, you quickly find yourself on autopilot, following these highways in your head. Attention switches into "energy save" mode, and fails to warn you when the rut no longer matches reality.

'I know I react defensively when he asks me why I'm doing things, but I feel like he is criticising me. Past boyfriends have done that a lot. Unfortunately, I bite back before I think about it and then it hurts him; then I feel bad, and we end up in this horrid cycle. It's the only problem in an otherwise perfect relationship, but it's harder to break this habit than I thought it would be.'

Attention goes to sleep when it slips into its ruts. Before you know it, you're on the same old road and missing the turn-off to a fresh and exciting one that beckons. It's impossible to create new pathways until you wake your attention up.

5. Re-Runs

'You literally saved my life. I was nearly strangled in the bedroom!' The group burst into fits of laughter, as the latest leadership program graduate shared his learnings. 'I used to lie in bed every night, re-running the day. Even when I tried to stop, it would just keep going. So I tried to drown out the noise of my own head by wearing headphones and listening to music. I would eventually drift off, only to wake in the middle of the night with the cord wrapped around my neck.' The laughter continued. 'But in all seriousness, when I realised I had set up a habit of re-running events that started in the morning and went all day, I could see what my problem was at night. I started by interrupting the habit throughout the day, and now I can report that I sleep soundly without music!'

Like a song set on repeat, events and conversations have a way of going around and around in your head. The more you replay them, the deeper you engrave them in your mind. Unfortunately, it tends to be the worrying and upsetting stories most people re-run. It feels like they take over whenever your attention is at a loose end, and you can find yourself stuck in the past, unable to let it go. Reflection is a great human capability from which you can learn and grow. But, reliving something that can't be changed, well after the lesson has been learnt, is a waste of precious attention—attention which could be used to turn back outward and set you on a path to a wiser and more fulfilling future.

6. 'Self Talk'

Your attention-grabbing thoughts can turn on you with vicious criticism: *You can't do that! You're not good enough. You're not a creative thinker. You should have known better.* These are common refrains for someone with a champion inner critic.

You pick these tapes up throughout life, and often in the earliest years. "You're a naughty boy" becomes an invitation to adopt the label and play the role. By the time you're out there living your adult life, you might be defining yourself by a series of random comments made by the people who've passed through your life. You pick them up from those closest to you, influential role models, even strangers. They're also implanted by the impressions gleaned from magazines, TV, cultural norms and unquestioned stereotypes.

'From the moment I look in the mirror each morning I am doing it: identifying all the things that are wrong. "You look old, you're getting grey, they'll see through you today, you're just not that good." My inner critic is like a radio station playing in the background, but no-one would tune into this station if they heard it. These are things I'd never even say to my worst enemy . . .'

If you give these labels attention, they grow. By tying your precious thread of connection to them so tightly, you mistakenly believe they define you completely, and you can no longer see yourself as you really are. Destructive "self talk" is the great saboteur, but it is a hollow narrator who should never be given the stage. There are other more worthy preachers, who speak the real truth, to invite into your head: *You are perfect. You are loved. You deserve a full life.*

7. Viruses

When you don't have control over your attention, the thoughts, intentions, moods and attitudes of others can hijack it. Soon you're doing what they're doing and feeling the way they feel. There is a scientific explanation for the source of these infectious viruses. Every person has a set of mirror neurons in their brain, whose role is to detect thoughts, emotions and behaviours in others, and respond as if you were experiencing them yourself. It's a handy way to learn from watching others and empathise with another's experience. But it also means you're susceptible to someone else's grumpy mood, mean spirit or campaign of revenge. Of course, happiness also spreads this way, which explains why a smile is hard to resist. But negative viruses have a tendency to invade quickly and deeply. If you're feeling irritable without good reason, maybe you've just picked it up like the common cold.

When you do have control over your attention, not only can you deftly avoid negative viruses, but you can also choose the ones you spread to others.

CONFESSIONS OF A MIND WANDERER > He was one of those people who looked like he was leading a desirable life. He lived in an idyllic location and had a wonderful wife and kids whom he adored. He was climbing the career ladder at work and he would say that he wanted for nothing. But despite all this, he often had a vacant look on his face. 'To be honest, I felt like a bystander watching my life pass by.' He realised that he was rarely really "there", usually dwelling on the past or wondering about the future. The idea of reviving his attention made so much sense. Within three weeks, he came bursting in the door with excitement. 'It's like my life is now in full colour. My surroundings are more vivid, sounds are sweeter and life is just more . . . vibrant!'

He went on to share how the connection with his children had changed. Before, he would play backyard cricket, but focus on everything his son was doing wrong and what he needed to do to get him into the school cricket team. He would chat with his kids at the dinner table, but also be re-running the day and wondering if he had made any mistakes. Once he woke up and started bringing his attention back to life, he started to see the things he'd been missing. When he really connected with his son, it was clear that he didn't even have a passion for cricket. He liked soccer! This opened up a whole new level of connection.

But the most powerful story was how it changed his relationship with his wife. 'My wife said I am as attentive as the person she met twenty-two years ago. We have fallen in love all over again. We're like teenagers!'

'I feel like I have plugged back into my life. Not my mind's interpretation of life, but what is actually there. It's just the small things. I see so much beauty and colour that had been there every single day, but I had failed to notice it. When you connect to the things outside of your head, you can't help but continue on your journey with a massive smile on your face.'

7 The Great Escape

IT WAS ALWAYS THERE > 'Stop, Mummy, stop!' She was already running late, and had used up all her negotiating chips to get her daughter this far. But her pint-sized, nature-loving child would be rushed no further. 'We must save him. You can't just run over him!' As she shared this story with her client, he nodded sympathetically. 'Happens to me all the time. No matter how well planned you think you are, kids are moving to a different beat. So how did you save him?' "Him" was a ladybird that her daughter had spotted on her way from the front door to the car. It was sitting very still on the driveway, but she insisted he was alive and must be gently removed from danger. 'Well, I was almost boiling over with frustration as I heaved everything into the car. But it was clear that the fastest way through this would be to join in, rather than resist. So I was dispatched to find a nice thin green leaf, while she kept her eye on him. Then she placed the leaf in front of him and moved it gently forward. When he slowly crawled onto the leaf, I had this sudden experience of things sort of coming to a standstill. All that existed was this amazing human so in touch with her world. It was a really magical moment.'

It's not surprising that children can lead you back to a connection with life. From the earliest of ages, they instinctively know how to use their attention well. They are endlessly curious, looking up to the sky and bending down to the ground. They will struggle forward in their stroller to follow the movements of a frolicking dog, they will point at big yellow trucks, they will stare at a stranger's face for longer than any adult would dare consider polite. They will ask you why, why and why again. Attention lays out the red carpet, welcoming ideas and experiences to the fertile open fields of their mind. These discoveries create their map of life.

Attention's great thrill is that it will never reveal the same thing twice. Children know this, finding just as much enjoyment in their twenty-fifth visit to the playground as they did in their first. They will run with open arms to greet you, only one hour after last seeing you. They want you to read them the same book each night for months. They will see shapes in clouds, nests in trees, and spot a change in the shop windows that you drive past each day.

Give me a child until he is seven and I will give you the man. This Jesuit motto is a surprisingly accurate estimate of the most significant phase in human learning. A child's brain increases in size fourfold in the preschool years, reaching 90 percent of the volume of the adult brain by the time they are six years old.[22] This process is called "exuberance"—a delightful word for the amazing natural development that creates a brain as unique as the face that it sits behind. This growth comes from the huge doses of life that flow through a child's open and very present attention.

But eventually, this burst of intensive early learning settles into a slower rhythm. Attention is freed up from its main task of making new connections, and turns to the task of strengthening those already formed. If you think your emerging teenager is becoming a bit opinionated, you're right! Their attention becomes less interested in the things that enthralled the child, and instead wanders more to what they think of the world passing in front of them. It is the inner world of attitudes, judgements, preferences and beliefs that absorbs them more.

Attention seesaws its way like this to maturity. But just like the child at the playground who straddles the middle of an undulating ride, trying to bring both sides into balance, the goal surely is to use all of attention's attributes throughout your life: to be present and to be reflective, to remain open but also be selective, and to recognise that discipline is the foil for freedom.

THE SWEET SPOT > Attention has a sweet spot. You find it when attention is kept moving smoothly, directed to things that can be well satisfied by its touch. Engaged in productive and meaningful action, it is open, receptive and calmly vigilant. It moves from one matter of genuine interest to the next with discipline and clarity, easily seeing through the tricks and traps laid by muggers, thieves and attention grabbers. You can feel yourself making headway, and you can see the difference you are making. It feels very different to the turmoil of attention bouncing wildly, or the fog of attention lost or captured. In this sweet spot you are energised and, rather than chewing up attention's power, it is renewed. A person in the sweet spot might be busy, but they are not "busy-minded". That makes all the difference.

'I'm always amazed how calm she is. She juggles so many things in this hectic environment and has her head around it all. The only time I've ever seen her frazzled was when a call came through in the middle of the shift, saying her daughter had fallen at school. It wasn't serious, but you could see the pieces she had been holding together in her head start to topple one by one. Basically she'd lost the flow, so they pulled her out and put someone else in charge until the shift ended.'

Attention is fragile, a house of cards where just one unexpected jolt can bring the whole thing crashing down. But it's also incredibly adaptable. It won't issue a complaint when you assault it; it won't cry foul when you trip it up. It will just obediently learn the moves you put it through, then repeat them as often as you like. It gets better and better at whatever you let it practise, until you hardly need to oversee its performance. Attention will not distinguish between a good or bad habit. It will not flash up a sign warning you that it has been too long since its last connection with life. And so you will not notice if, slowly, one moment at a time, your attention becomes lost in the wilderness. But you are transported there too, inseparable partners through good and bad.

If this has been your journey, you're not alone. Pick up any study that explores how people feel about their workload, their life balance, or their time management, and they universally reveal a glaring problem: we feel more overwhelmed, stressed and anxious than ever before. Worst of all, we feel trapped. The seesaw is being held down on one side and it feels like there is no balance, no relief and no lightness. That's what happens when the fragile thread of your attention is tethered to an endless to-do list, twisted in knots of worry, and shackled to "always-on" technology. You feel like a prisoner, as surely as if you have been locked away.

When you're trapped, you naturally turn to thoughts of escape. The freedom glimpsed through the bars of your cell taunts you cruelly and you'll try anything to break out. But are you searching for your freedom in the right places? Can you find your way back to the sweet spot from here? On the path to reclaiming a full life, you will be tempted by many strategies that promise the world but, like the latest fad diets, deliver only short-term results. It can leave you more disillusioned, more overwhelmed and more anxious.

ZONING OUT > While working your attention too hard, too fast and for too long can ruin it, so can backing off too much. Attention is not revived by dropping out of "hyper drive", to drift aimlessly. That's like tipping the seesaw from one side to the other. In neither of these places can attention connect you to life, or nourish the things you care for most. Sitting blankly in front of the TV, grabbing a drink to take the edge off, indulging in a bit of retail therapy, or zoning out to music might all block out the frantic busyness of the day for a while. But if all you've done is leave your attention at a loose end to ruminate over re-runs, what ifs or worries, then you've swapped one prison for another.

'So what did I miss?' she asked as she flopped down beside him on the couch. 'Oh, I wasn't watching it.' She'd been dragged away by a phone call right in the middle of her favourite TV show, and was hoping he could fill her in. But even though he hadn't moved, and his eyes were clearly looking forward, his mind had been elsewhere. 'Sorry, I was just going over some things that happened at work today.'

When you take your hands off the wheel, attention will grasp this moment of freedom as an opportunity to slip into its comfortable old habits. Unless you've been actively training it to return to a calm centre when busyness subsides, it's more likely to slip into another form of the busy, flighty or circling actions it finds most familiar. For many people, sitting alone without any form of distraction is a torture. Their attention finds these wide open spaces daunting and uncomfortable. Just look at the people waiting in line at a bank, waiting for their takeaway coffee order, or even waiting the few seconds it takes for the light to turn green at a crossing. Heads are down in mobile devices, rather than up watching the world passing by. If you're escaping the office to clear your head, and doing anything other than walking with your eyes up and your senses turned out to your environment, you are still imprisoned.

Ironically, the great escape from mobile technology is driving the development of a whole new class of technological solutions. After a short burst of rapid growth, people are opting out of open social media sites and switching to closed networks, where they can limit the constant flow of information. Some of the most popular apps promise to filter the ceaseless noise and save you from this overwhelming task. But if you've already got a busy mind, losing this daily distraction can trigger even more anxiety. An interesting study found that a large proportion of people would rather give themselves a mild electric shock, than sit without distraction and only their own thoughts for fifteen minutes.[23] It's no surprise that digital detox retreats have emerged, even for young children—a service no-one could have foreseen just a few years ago.

If you think you can save your attention by shutting down technology, that's only part of the battle. A device-free hour for the family is only valuable if that hour is used to reconnect to each other or other valued life experiences. Keeping your phone next to the bed, but switching off the alert tones, might give you longer periods of unbroken sleep, but it will not stop your attention from seeking it out the moment you wake. Turning off your email system's automatic download while you're working on an important project won't stop you clicking the update button for fear of missing something. Even with devices off and out of reach, if your attention searches for their familiar face, you are still a slave to the master.

The struggle to escape the flood is in full swing. Yet we fiddle while Rome burns. The quick fix is taking over the world. As attention struggles to stay with one thing for very long at all, new ways of working, entertaining and selling emerge. If you find it too difficult to read 400 words, you'll be pleased to hear that microblogging is replacing blogging. Maybe you can cope with 140 characters? You'll get a buzz of attention, a tick of approval, a share, then we can all move to the next important message. But instead of reviving the health of your attention, you're adapting the world to match the moves of your ailing attention, and it's unsustainable. It's a rush to the bottom, and the ones who get there first realise they have become like sparrows picking crumbs from the path. This is not the way back to life.

THE TRADE-OFF > Facebook Post, 7 September, 6.44am:
Attention is a precious gift, but in a busy life we often withhold it from those who need it most. Who deserves the gift of your attention today?

Comment, 7 September, 6.45am:
I'm going to give it to ME.

When the worries of daily life, the pressures of work, the needs of the family, and the endless to-do list push themselves forward, the attention trade-off begins. But the dominoes fall quickly. You're the first victim, cutting back on your sleep, cancelling your exercise, and deferring your "me time". Once you've traded your own space, you start eating into the moments of connection with those you care for most. The kids' bedtime story is too often missed, you settle for watching a video of the school concert because you just can't get there, an anniversary dinner is put off and the annual Christmas catch-up with friends will have to wait until New Year.

There's an implied assumption that one day soon you will be able to trade it all back again, but this never happens. "Once I get on top of things" is a promised land that few will ever reach. All you've done is stop giving attention to the things that matter in life, and soon you will be wondering where the meaning went. You thought you made a deal that would bring you back to the light one day, but it was a gamble that didn't pay off.

'Just an update to let everyone know I left my job last week. Freaking out, but found one silver lining: I picked the kids up from school for the first time this year, then did homework with them. I'm thinking about volunteering for tuckshop duty!' It's often life's curveballs that give you pause to recognise how large the price you have been paying for attention trade-offs really is.

Even then, many people see these situations not as an opportunity to start afresh, but as another burden to be carried by their exhausted attention. 'I've asked my ex to keep the kids with her for a few weeks, while I work out what I'm going to do next. I can't believe how many people are telling me to do the opposite and take a week away with the kids. I don't know how they think I could waste this time that I should be using to find a new job.'

We must all trade off one activity for another, meaning that you make choices every day about what will get your attention. If the phone rings while you are drafting a letter, the act of taking the call is a choice to remove your attention from the letter, and the act of ignoring the call is a choice to continue with your letter. But it's rarely that clear-cut. It's usually more like this:

The alarm went off to remind her of the team meeting. She just wanted to finish the last paragraph of her long email, so she put her head down and rushed quickly through the words. A few minutes later her secretary stuck her head in the door. 'Are you going to that meeting?' She jumped up 'Yes, yes. I just wanted to get this out to everyone before they go home tonight.' She quickly read the email through one more time, then pushed the send button. As she rushed out the door, she suddenly remembered that she'd promised to copy a colleague into that email, and she wheeled back, clicking quickly on the "sent items" folder. 'Why does it always take so long to appear!' Impatiently, she grabbed her smartphone to send her daughter an SMS confirming what time she would pick her up from work on her way home. As she clicked away, another SMS arrived, and she could see it was from her best friend, who lived overseas. 'Guess what? I'm coming back home for a whole month, so we'll have lots of time to catch up. I have important news.' She felt a thrill of excitement at the thought of seeing her friend, but then she felt sudden dread. 'I wonder what's wrong? She wouldn't leave her job for that long unless something is wrong. Maybe she's lost her job. Or maybe she's sick! Oh dear, I can't stand not knowing!' She was half way through tapping an urgent response demanding to know the "important news", when her secretary came bursting in. 'Why are you still here? They've been waiting for fifteen minutes. I thought you were on your way. They've sent a search party out!!'

As she rushed to the elevator, her mind was a complete muddle. She hadn't sent the SMS to her daughter, or to her friend. She hadn't copied her colleague in on the email, and she'd left her folder behind. She arrived at the team meeting with her head down and only her smartphone in hand. With all eyes on her, she mumbled an apology, and asked if someone had a spare copy of the agenda. As it was slid across in front of her, she heaved a heavy sigh and started the meeting.

If you end the day with little to show for your overwhelming busyness, you'd be forgiven for thinking it was all a big waste of time. So it's no surprise that most people believe time is the threatened resource, the lost prize, and the key to freedom. But attention and time are very, very different. All the free time in the world cannot save your fragile attention, when it's being pushed and pulled in too many directions.

In fact, a bit of free time can reveal how lost your attention just might be. 'I finally went for that massage and I spent the whole time re-running the week. I had all these ideas about how I could improve my team, but now I can't remember any of them!'

When you are lost in thought, sucked down the vortex by an alluring device, or waylaid by an attention thief on your way to an important event, time keeps marching on. You only lose time when you first lose attention. 'Sorry I'm late again! I was searching for some research on the internet and I came across a site that had interviews with people who had been involved in the experiments. It was really fascinating, but I just lost track of time. Did I miss anything?'

Time is unstoppable, unalterable, inexorably moving forward at the same pace for us all. It is not time itself that is precious, but your experience of the time that you have in this life. Only attention can give you this.

UNPLUGGED > Anything that unplugs you from life will bring only temporary relief. It is sometimes necessary to do this, when you realise you are plugged into a socket that is draining your energy and returning nothing to you. But until you plug your attention back into a new source, it cannot reconnect you to life. Too many people get caught up in the plan of escape, running away from the pressures of life, but then find themselves right back in the same place again.

'I need that retreat each year. By the time I get there I'm a mess, but I feel great when I leave, ready to face the storm again. I've detoxed, started meditating, and made a commitment to take a mini-break every month. Of course, that first week back is the big test. There's always heaps of email to catch up on, and all the things I put off before I went away. It's hard to get these new healthy habits in place in that environment.

To be honest, the longest I've stuck to my fresh new lifestyle is about two months . . .' It's also a familiar story for the large proportion of people who make a New Year's resolution each year but don't quite achieve it.

For some people, the escape plan is even more radical. Corporate refugees flee the tyranny of big business for the ultimate sea change: their own small business, working for a not-for-profit, taking over the child rearing, moving to the country, even moving countries. The dream is eventually replaced by reality and, instead of the known pressures, familiar but wearing, your attention must now turn itself to new challenges. Uncertainty, new learning, unmet expectations, loss of support networks, meeting new people, loss of status, unfamiliar quietness, new tastes, sounds, sights . . . Attention is freed from the old shackles, but is it up to the challenge of rebuilding its health, while you're also finding your feet in a new life. Some people eventually feel the freedom emerge, as they shed old habits and get past the shock of change. For others, it does not bring the promised freedom, but a set of new worries to replace the old ones. They have freed the body but their attention remains imprisoned.

THE ESCAPE IS HERE > The growing popularity of spiritual workshops, yoga, and meditation reflects the dawning realisation that reclaiming a full life demands that work be done at a very fine level. It's not a physical escape that is needed, but one where you dive in more fully to life.

It's why mindfulness is the new black. Over the last decade, it has found its way into classrooms, retirement homes, mining camps and boardrooms. It's a popular response to growing concerns about wellbeing, resilience and productivity. Yet many who search desperately for relief from the sense of being overwhelmed skirt around it, preferring a retreat, a holiday or a device-free hour. It's time to get over the aversion, the cynicism, the doubts and misconceptions, and recognise that the gift of attention is only a present when you are present.

Being present is a simple act. You were born an expert in paying attention to the present, and you have lived the joy that it brings at some point in your life. But those early years of clear, open, full attention may seem a distant memory, if you've been training your attention to be anywhere but the present. Like a person who has let their health and fitness take back seat to a career for many years, suddenly you look in the mirror and do not recognise the weary person looking back. But rather than being daunted by the feeling that the road back to yourself will be as long and rocky as the road that brought you here, take heart. It takes just one moment to revive the dying art of paying attention.

Let attention join with your senses. They are the true guides back to your body, where the present always is. In the moment of tasting your food, you are present. In the moment of seeing the wide open blue sky, you are connected. In the moment of hearing your child's laugh, your love will flow. In each moment of connection with the present, attention is gathered into a strong and clear stream, dropping all other matters.

'I drive past a park on the way to work and, every time I pass by, I feel like pulling over and sitting on the grass for five minutes. But I've always got too much to do and it just sounds a bit silly.' But one day he overcame the uneasiness of calling a pause in his busy day and did it. Before long, his little break in nature became his most powerful performance tool. 'Whenever I am blocked for ideas or need inspiration, I just go and sit on the park bench opposite the office and the ideas come. I am three times more productive than I used to be and less stressed, that's for sure. But I also seem more able to create time for others. People who I was too busy to talk to now get priority.'

Your brain suffers fatigue when you work for long periods without a break, particularly on tasks that require intense concentration. Research supports the fact that connecting with your senses is powerful, and that taking in the sights and sounds of nature can be especially beneficial for your brain. Performances in attention and memory tests improve by 20 percent after subjects walk through a park. The same results were not achieved when walking down a busy street.[24] And it seems that paying attention to nature does more than improve your productivity. It lifts your mood and makes you feel better. It also makes people behave better. People who spend more time in natural environments value their community and close relationships more highly, and are more generous with money.[25]

It is here in the present that your attention connects you to life. It is only from here in the present that you can give the gift of your attention to others. It is here in the present that another's gift to you is received. The crossroad of your flowing stream of attention with mine, and with every other person's on this planet, is here—always here. If you want to revive the dying art of paying attention, not just for yourself but to save this endangered resource for future generations, start by being present.

'It's such a relief to hear you talk about finding moments in the day to pay attention. Just last weekend, I was trying to work out whether it was possible for me to achieve the goal of 10,000 hours meditation in my lifetime. I've been going for two years now with twenty minutes morning and night, so I figure it's another forty years, give or take. I don't think I'll make it . . .'

The measure of 10,000 hours has been touted as the amount of practice required to achieve mastery in a field. Whether it's performing at the elite level in sport, music, chess, computer programming or meditation, those who perform at the very highest level have a history of deliberate practice. But don't set yourself an unrealistic goal that hangs like a cruel mirage, somewhere just out of reach. You live in the real world. There will be distractions. Your mind will wander. But every single moment of intentional choice to gather up your fragmented attention, and bring it back to a place of connection, will strengthen your attention. It is not just the chunks of intensive practice that count when building a skill. Every moment counts.

To connect with life, for just one moment more than you might otherwise have done today, brings you one step closer to living a full life. In fact, in that moment you **are** living a full life. These moments of full attention are when real life happens, how memories are made, and where one more drop of care falls to nourish the parched ground. You can revive the dying art of paying attention well before attaining 10,000 hours of practice. Just start with one moment, please.

MOMENTS OF PRESENCE > So what is "one moment"? A simple dictionary definition, from Merriam-Webster online, is: *A minute portion or comparatively brief period of time.* But you might be surprised to hear there is a formal definition, albeit a medieval one, based on sundials. Because of the way time was measured between sunrise and sunset, there were forty moments in a solar hour. One moment, by medieval measure, is equivalent to ninety seconds.

In reality, there is a good argument for setting yourself any goal from nine to ninety seconds, when it comes to reviving the dying art of paying attention. Make it too short and you might be taking credit for the accidental jolt your attention receives from a loud noise or strong smell. Just because you notice the sunset when someone else points it out, does not mean you have undertaken the conscious act of giving it your full attention. If there is no conscious awareness or intentional choice in what your attention does, then you probably haven't strengthened your attention at all. Only you can know the truth, but the feeling of completeness and pure presence is your guide. That is the return you experience when attention connects, and you are plugged into life.

Anything longer than six to ten seconds will give you a run for your money, because it's about then that attention makes its move to slip back to a favourite habit, notice a distraction, or jump on a passing thought. It's completely natural for it to do this, just as it's natural for your lungs to move in and out. Your goal is not to hold attention fixed or rigid, but to gently steer its roaming movements wisely. As you strengthen your attention fitness, what you are really strengthening is how quickly you notice it take flight, how conscious you are of where it has wandered, and your ability to gently return it back to the present. That is a powerful skill, and that is the art of paying attention.

For those with a greater desire to master the art of paying attention, you might take your lead from experts in other fields. Aim for periods of longer deliberate practice by taking a meditation class. This is similar to taking yourself to the gym each day, when you want to boost your health and fitness. It's a proactive strategy to strengthen muscles and enhance aerobic capacity, but it is not the whole picture. If, when you leave the gym, you light up a cigarette, load up on hamburgers, and head for the local bar, you will undo many of the benefits you gained from your practice. Likewise, if you meditate daily in a quiet private spot, then spend the next twelve hours allowing your attention to go to "crazy-town", being pushed and pulled by attention muggers, agitated and annoyed by attention thieves, and stressed and frustrated by harmful attention grabbers, your reserve of attention stability will quickly end up in the red. Moments of returning to the present throughout the day are key to breaking destructive habits that threaten your precious attention.*

The very act of directing your attention through one of your senses, to connect fully with the world around you, can be seen in the brain. In just a few short weeks of mindfulness practice, your experience of fear and stress can be diminished, and this reveals itself as a physical change in your brain. Dwelling less on worries and negativities means that the amygdala (the part of the brain alert to danger, that drives the body's stress response) shrinks. Diverting activity instead to the pre-frontal cortex (responsible for awareness and decision-making) means that this area is strengthened. The simple discipline of noticing where your attention is, and consciously redirecting it, boosts your

---

* Meditation traditions offer a much richer experience than simple attention training. By watching where your mind wanders, what it grasps, and what captures it, you enter a deeper form of self-awareness. Building attention stability is just the first step in most traditions, but committing to meditation can offer many layers of realisation about the true nature of your existence, and can bring deeply fulfilling results.

impulse control, that most crucial skill for navigating through distractions.

This is just one positive result from a number of emerging studies, revealing that healthy attention forms the basis for life's most fulfilling experiences.[26] The ability to return your attention to the present, giving it a break from tight and tiring focused activity, is also the key to creativity, self-awareness and insight—all those things that cannot be done when attention is bouncing quickly across the surface of life. People report feeling more productive, noticing things with greater clarity and being more in control of their emotions.

It works because, at the most basic level, the action that sits at the core of all mindfulness practices is one that gently trains your attention to return from its wanderings and come home. Whether you're guiding it smoothly past the inviting doorway of a hypnotising device, or drawing it back from the wasteland of worrying thoughts, this simple act of getting in the driver's seat and making conscious choices is the first step towards nourishing this precious resource and giving it a chance to do its thing.

Your attention will rest in the present for just a moment, before it notices an arising thought or a passing distraction. Those things will always come, and attention will always wander. The art of paying attention is truly the art of wise choices. And these choices are made on a moment-to-moment basis.

Life is only here, in the present. If you want to connect with life, your attention must come to the present. You cannot change the past or control the future. When you dwell on those things you miss out on life. A moment of full attention, flowing from you to nourish those things you care for most, is the only thing that life asks. Once the currency of care flows,

– ONE MOMENT PLEASE –

life blooms around you. The smile of a stranger as you enter an elevator; your granddaughter's soft hand in yours as she walks by your side; a genuine hug from your ageing father; the unexpected flavours on your dinner plate; the sound of distant birds calling to each other; a golden line tracing the clouds as the sun sets. And like a child once more, you realise that attention will never reveal the same thing twice. Every moment is different in so many subtle ways, and only attention can expose this truth.

Yesterday is history.
Tomorrow is a mystery.
Today is a gift.
That's why it is called the present.
ANON

8 Wise Investments

BRAIN TRAPS > We live in a world of contradictions. We care about happiness, but spend time dwelling on worries and frustrations. We care about our loved ones, but allow our to-do list to come before the act of just being there with them. We care about our friends, but only half listen when they tell us what's going on in their lives. We care about living a life of meaning, but fill the space for deep reflection with busy activity.

We're like kids in a candy store, spoilt for choice. Surrounded by an endless selection of things just itching to get our attention, the choice is overwhelming, almost sickening. In fact, it **is** making us sick. Stress, anxiety, loneliness, guilt, confusion and disappointment are the symptoms, and an empty life is the result. It's ironic that living in a world with so much to offer has left us feeling like we have less, rather than more. But it's clear that the things we are adding to life are just pushing out those things that make life worth living. There's more candy on the shelf but, rather than opening us up, this shuts us down, disabling our ability to choose wisely.

When it comes to attention, more is less. We become paralysed in the face of too many choices. If you've ever stood in a shopping aisle, trying to decide which laundry detergent to buy when your usual choice has been removed, you know this is true. More choices do not make us happier, they add to the sense of being overwhelmed. Companies are beginning to understand that they can boost their sales by reducing their range, making it easier for your attention to take in the necessary information and land on a decision. The same can be said for life. Poking through the clouds are just a few things that make life worth living, and the rest is pure distraction.

Gathering attention up into a stream that connects you to the present is just the first step in reviving the dying art of paying attention. With renewed impulse control, stability and depth, attention yearns to enter into a valued exchange. But how do you know which choices are the right ones?

We have forever been driven to move towards reward, and to move away from threat. It's a fundamental operating principle of the brain, and one that has served humanity well. Until now. It is almost impossible to distinguish a reward from a threat in this complex modern world; a simple measure like "what feels good" doesn't work, when it comes to choosing where to give your attention. For example, habits are comfortable, and when you go "off habit", your brain screams out a warning. When you slip back into your ruts, you are rewarded with the soothing feeling that all is right again, regardless of whether the habit is good for you or bad for you. It's a trap that keeps you on the treadmill, living the same day over and over again, and missing the opportunities to create your best life.

Your brain's reward centres are fickle, giving you a zap of delight for all sorts of things that will not bring harmony to your life. You'll feel it when you engage in intrigue and gossip. It's triggered when you score a point against a foe. It keeps you returning in anticipation of a win at the gaming tables. It will take you shopping for things you really don't need. It tempts you to do just one more thing on the to-do list, rather than stop and play with the kids. It is addicted to the sympathy offered when you play the victim. It makes you feel important when you hear a message arrive on your device, and when you get a like, a share or any reaction that shows you were noticed. But you have been conned. The burst of "feel good" drugs are an unreliable guide through life's maze.

ATTENTION GIVERS > Unlike the short burn and fizzle of self-gratification, wisely-invested attention ignites an intense, warming glow that awakens a deep sense of fulfilment. This is true reward, registered not only deep within your brain, but felt through an open heart, and experienced as a freedom of spirit. It is a return that only a handful of life's choices can deliver, but they are the ones that you will recognise as enduring sources of happiness. Countless philosophers and generations of homespun wisdoms align with brain science, to reveal that there are certain things that form the foundation of a good life. Being present, being purposeful, being positive and being with people are the enduring points of connection with life. It is with each of these that your attention grows stronger, that you are revitalised, and that meaning finds its way back into your life. When attention is released from the bonds that hold it back, you will find that these are the things you most naturally turn towards.

'A big holiday away from it all always changes your perspective. It took me one week just to slow down. I couldn't believe how fast I was walking, and how on edge I felt. I almost jumped with fright every time I heard a mobile phone. I didn't even have mine with me, but I was reaching for it constantly and felt anxious about what I might be missing. The second week I started to sleep longer. Instead of jumping up and marching through each little village like I was on a mission to invade it, all I wanted to do was sit at a cafe and watch the passing parade. Watching the simple play of life was fascinating and, after a few days, I could feel myself moving at the same pace. By week three, I was questioning the habits I had built up in my life. There was evidence all around me that the version of life I had been living was only one option. I realised there were lots of things I needed to change, when I went home. I was doing too many things that just filled up space but meant nothing. In fact, I could see very clearly what had been holding me back. It was just the clutter of life and, when it fell away, I could see a path forward again for the first time in ages.'

BEING PURPOSEFUL > *Why am I here?* This is one of life's big questions. A deep desire to feel that we have made a difference is wired into the brain. Altruism, whether it be giving to charity, being of service to others or performing a random act of kindness, gives as great a reward to the giver as it does to the receiver. The hypothesis is that helping each other in an interdependent society will enhance our own chance of survival, so the brain rewards the action.[27]

– WISE INVESTMENTS –

While you may never be able to track a direct return to yourself of any specific tangible gain, opening the flow of attention up by investing a generous dose of it, whenever the opportunity opens in front of you, is a powerful act that can enliven your family, your company, your community and beyond. The flood of feel-good chemicals that rush from the brain has physical benefits. Volunteering has been shown to lower depression and enhance wellbeing, and is associated with a 22 percent reduction in the risk of premature death.[28] Acting for the good of the whole is a compelling proposition.

'I just felt a surge of sympathy for the people I saw on TV. They only live one suburb away from me, and I was sitting in bright sunshine while their homes were being flooded. When I heard that people were on the march, I grabbed my gumboots and joined in.' He was recalling his experience as part of the Mud Army, a spontaneous community of volunteers who took action without being asked, after a flood hit his local city. He even took a week off work and spent twelve hours each day helping complete strangers to clean their homes and recover what they could. Trudging through mud with his arms deep in rubbish, his spirits were high. 'Work didn't even enter my mind, and my stress dropped away. I ended the week feeling energised and really fulfilled. I still feel good when I drive through those streets, like I'm really part of a community. It was a lesson for me about being less self-absorbed, so I make a point now of doing more community service activities throughout the year.'

Being purposeful protects your precious attention from one of the great traps of our time. As busyness of mind grows, you may notice that many of your daily thoughts are about yourself: *Do I like this? What do they think about me? I wonder what this will do for*

- 1 1 7 -

me. I prefer something else. These are circling thoughts that hold your attention in close, and hold it back from a connection with life. While it's tempting to judge everything you come across through the tinted glasses of your own preferences, assumptions and past experiences, these will taint your view of the world and waste precious attention. Such circling "me-oriented" thinking is also strongly associated with anxiety and depression.

We exist as part of a series of interconnected communities, systems that rise or fall as a direct result of our collective acts. Being purposeful means setting aside your own perspective and taking a moment to consider needs other than your own. Asking yourself, 'What is the real need here?' is very different to asking yourself, 'What do I want here?' The distinction can redirect your precious attention towards the very place where a meaningful life awaits you.

This connection with needs beyond your own may manifest in different ways for each person. For some, it is found in a faith or a spiritual philosophy that offers guidance on how to maintain this open and giving attention. Again, brain science shows that spiritual belief lights up the brain in particular ways,[29] explaining the strong sense of meaning and fulfilment that this path through life can offer. But for others, a source of purposeful connection is found closer to home.

'I struggled with my role as a parent. I realised that I was smothering them, because I was scared of all the horrible things that can happen out there. My attention was not always a loving form of attention; it was often controlling and confining. Suddenly, I saw that they were worrying about things that kids shouldn't even think about, and I knew that had something to do with my own anxieties. One day I heard someone talk about what they thought their purpose was as a parent. It was to create an environment in which children could grow, becoming resilient and happy individuals. They had removed the concept of "my children" and this had made their parenting so much stronger and more conscious. I realised this was the thing that was missing for me. I was being driven by my fears and not seeing these children in their full light, as humans in my care for a short time. Now I ask myself each day, "What do they need today, to grow into the person they have the potential to be?" While my fears are there, they no longer dictate my choices.'

You don't need an answer to the big question of why you are here to be purposeful. Every activity has a purpose. Simply asking yourself, 'Why is this important?' will either reveal a deep and motivating reason to continue giving it your precious attention, or a reason to stop. Organisations with clear purpose offer their people a powerful tool. In the clutter generated by competing demands for attention, to bring to mind your organisational purpose will bring clarity to your priorities. The most everyday types of companies can become businesses of true service, when they are inspired by purpose.

What purpose underpins your organisation? Why does it exist? The answer will provide your attention with a strong point of connection, which will help you navigate the plethora of *What? How? When? Who? Where?* questions that can bog you down.

When you live purposefully, attention is less vulnerable to the shallow, passing fancies that seek to steal a piece of it. With your sights set higher, your attention learns to unfurl further into the world, and, through it, the best in you can reach out to the places where the world can be changed by your touch.

BEING POSITIVE > There is a science of happiness. It tells us that 40 percent of your happiness is within your control and not dictated by life circumstances.[30] It tells us that the ratio of positive to negative experiences required to perform well is 3:1.[31] It tells us that when you focus on your strengths, rather than dwelling on your weaknesses, you are 12.5 percent more productive.[11] It seems that wherever you look, positive emotions drive performance, success and fulfilment.

It is more nourishing for attention to play in a field of possibility than a den of despair. Being positive opens attention widely to the world and lets the currency of care flow. You become more curious and interested, more caring and responsive, and more easily connected. But a focus on negatives reveals very different behaviours. Not only is the observable activity in the brain very different, but the chemicals that flood the body have a very different effect. Negativity triggers feelings of stress, fear or even anger. Rather than flowing generously, attention becomes captured by the negativity and anchored in a dark place.

It was the end of another busy week and she sat down to read the feedback forms from a presentation she had given to a group earlier that day. *Not as engaging as I would have hoped.* This one simple comment cut deep, and she re-ran it all weekend. The other forty-nine forms were overwhelmingly positive but, instead of focusing on those, she chose to give her attention to the one person who wasn't engaged. 'I'll never do one of those sessions again,' she told her husband. So the light she offered the world by sharing her story was dimmed, not by the person who made the comment, but by her own choice to give this one perspective the power to break her spirit.

– WISE INVESTMENTS –

What you focus on grows. It is not your circumstances that define your life, but your choices. While we casually say, 'There are two sides to every story,' the fact is that every situation has many facets and we all choose our own perspective. Your brain is literally shaped by those things that get your attention. Neural pathways that trace out an experience with more colour around the positive elements will find it easier to discover the same patterns and colours the next day, and vice versa.

Unfortunately, negatives grab your attention so much more quickly and strongly than positives. For this reason, they also pervade the environment and infiltrate your thinking in devious ways. The nightly news and current affairs programs suck you in, by playing to this negativity bias. Political campaigners use negative advertising, because it is known to have greater influence over swinging voters. Business meetings dwell on risks and threats, often for much longer than it takes to devise a plan to manage them.

This begs not only the question about what this does to your own attention over time, but what it is doing to the flow of attention through our communities, our nations and the world. If you only look for war and hatred, you will find it and start believing it is all that exists. If you only look for reasons why someone is not performing to your expectations, any positive results they deliver will go barely noticed. If you only look for the path of cutbacks and retreat as the business world changes, you will be the last to see the new opportunities that open up with every paradigm shift.

Emotions are contagious. If you're being infected by negatives, it is even more crucial that you take a moment to make very clear and intentional choices about where you give your attention. Because positive emotions are also contagious—even a smile from a stranger can change your mood. But it is attention that allows this force to flow from one to another. This does not mean you have to discard all negative people from your life, but you must make a conscious choice to not let their perspective invade your attention. In fact, you can even be a force for good, by thinking more about the viruses you spread to others.

In an interesting experiment to test whether one person's state of mind could affect another's, the "happiest person in the world", a Buddhist monk, was brought together with one of the unhappiest people, a university professor. As they engaged in a discussion, their biological markers were monitored. The professor displayed all the signs of high agitation as the discussion started, but during the first fifteen minutes he became calmer, eventually matching the state of the Buddhist monk. Attention has the power to transform.

'Our boss came back from his leadership program a changed man. He was always so busy before. If you needed to speak with him he was helpful, but got things over quickly and got you out the door. Now he stops whatever he is doing and comes around the desk to sit next to you. There's eye contact and you feel more welcome. But the most striking thing is that he seems to have grown a personality! I thought he was a really serious guy, but he is funny. The mood in the team is really different, and we're powering through the work so much more effectively. I am enjoying coming to work more than I have in years.'

Positive experiences within a team will genuinely lift perform-ance. But this does not mean you must make everything light and cheery. It just means approaching people in a way that opens them up, rather than shutting them down. A leader's greatest

— WISE INVESTMENTS —

challenge is to be conscious of the impact they are having on people's attention. Positive feedback will lift their spirits, but the experience of receiving difficult feedback can also be positive. Everything from your demeanour, tone of voice and choice of language will have an impact, but it is your open and clear flow of attention that expresses what is needed most: care, support and encouragement. While a ratio of three positive experiences to each negative one has been identified as the goal for team success, optimal performance emerges when the team experiences a ratio of 6:1.[32]

One of the greatest barriers to achieving this positive focus in the workplace is the tendency to give more attention to what's going wrong than what's going right. Many businesses believe that, if they attend thoroughly to risks, weaknesses and problems, they will be able to eliminate them. It leaves little energy to explore opportunities, strengths and possibilities. This can create a risk-averse culture, a blame culture, or one where people are simply unwilling to act. But culture is just a reflection of what's happening at the individual level. That's why leadership is so important. If every individual is encouraged to turn their own attention to what **can** be done, whole institutions can be transformed without massive and costly structural change programs.

Simply being aware of your strengths can boost your productivity by 7.8 percent; focusing on them every day lifts this figure to 12.5 percent. But the benefits of giving more attention to your strengths go deeper. Using your strengths improves health and wellness outcomes. The more hours that people use their strengths during a day, the less they report experiencing worry, stress, anger, sadness or even physical pain.[11] The power of small moments given to being positive is undeniable.

One of the most effective exercises for lifting your own personal ratio is the expression of gratitude. 'I write down three things I am grateful for each day before I go to bed. I've noticed a big change in my mood in just one month. The idea sounded a bit fluffy when I first heard it, but there is no doubt it has changed what my attention is drawn to during the day. In the beginning, I had to look hard to find something. But once I realised it's as simple as noticing how nice the day is, someone holding the door open for me, or that I'm lucky enough to have healthy parents, it became easy. I've set the challenge that I must identify something different each day, and I haven't been stumped yet. I can't recommend this strategy more highly for anyone who thinks the world is all doom and gloom, like I did.'

Thoughts, people, places, books, movies, rituals, habits, food, exercise, behaviours, emotions, intentions and activities all affect your attention and define your life. Being positive is a choice that becomes easier and easier. It's about recognising that what you give your attention to in any moment can shut you down or open you up. There's no doubt which feels better, and there's no doubt which connects you with those things in life that matter the most.

BEING WITH PEOPLE > At the end of your life, the things you will wish you had given your precious attention to will become clear. In *The Top Five Regrets of the Dying*, author Bronnie Ware reminds us of one of life's lessons that you have heard before: we will wish we had spent more time with the people who matter to us most. Connecting with another person is the truest and most real form of attention exchange. You will experience a physical lift when you receive the gift of attention from another,

– WISE INVESTMENTS –

and you will see the positive effects when yours hits its mark. Surely this is where attention needs to flow most, and where it will thrive and grow. And it's not only those you love and care for who deserve this precious gift. Those who are often invisible might need it more: the shopkeeper, the bus driver, or the homeless person you just walked past. We are all boosted by a moment of connection, and the flow-on effects can be powerful.

He was fourteen and completely lost. The weight of responsibility was too great a burden on his young shoulders, and he saw no way to escape but to follow the path of rebellion. Underage drinking unleashed a raging temper, and his destructive behaviour at school had driven his frustrated teachers to the edge. Suspension from school would be the next step, but he didn't care. He couldn't see a future for himself, so school was only a place to hide out during the day. But on this particular day, it had all become too hard to bear. He found himself lying on the classroom floor, secretly wishing it would swallow him up. He became conscious of the click of heels coming down the corridor and he braced for the consequences he knew would follow. But what came next was completely unexpected. As he sat in his boardroom twenty-three years later, telling his story to a room full of his peers, you could hear that the power of that moment was still as fresh as the day it happened.

'It was too quiet, so I opened my eyes and my English teacher was lying on the floor beside me. Instead of glaring at me with judgment and anger, her eyes were full of what I can only describe as love. She just whispered, "What can I do to help you?" and I was overwhelmed. It was a moment of pure kindness that I could never have foreseen; it's the moment that changed my life.' Three hours later, he was still sitting with his

– 1 2 5 –

teacher in the school canteen, sharing things he thought he would never tell anyone: the anxiety stirred by his mother's drinking, her sudden departure from their lives, his father's unpredictable temper, and finally, this second parent also walking out and leaving him to raise his two younger brothers alone. He would be forever grateful for the moment his teacher chose to lay on the floor beside him, rather than reprimand him. It was the only way he could have opened up, and it changed his life.

Attention works best when it's given freely, and when this flow can move unhindered between us all. You cannot underestimate the impact of a moment of connection with a random person on the street, nor should you anticipate what it might bring. If you play the important role of keeping the flow of attention moving, you have made a difference today. But all too often we are shutting it down. When you get caught up in your own private world, you sever the thread that unites us all.

'I feel uncomfortable giving eye contact. I don't like people looking at me and I know I use my computer and my phone as a shield to block that,' she began. Before she could continue, a usually timid team member interjected, 'I thought it was because you didn't like me, so I've been trying to stay out of your way.' It was an "aha moment" for this leader. She had been blocking the flow of attention, and it affected the team more than she had realised. But more importantly, she could see the cloud it had cast over this young woman. Suddenly she saw her not as a staff member, but as a fellow traveller through life, and she was saddened that her neglect had caused her pain.

Often it's just the clutter and distraction of busyness that hinders a genuine connection with others, but it's no excuse. 'I'm sorry I've been withholding attention from you over the last few weeks.' She had an important deadline and the work-load had been constant. But he had a different perspective. 'You don't need to apologise. I don't feel like you have neglected me at all. Yes, you've had to put more time into your work, but when you're with me, you give me your full attention. Whether it's ten hours, ten minutes or ten seconds, I always feel that you are completely there with me.'

Remember, time and attention are very different. A moment of full attention can deliver all the love in your heart, and it is this act that nourishes others and keeps the flow of healthy attention moving between us all.

But busyness is not the only cause of disconnection from others. If you are disconnected from yourself, the flow is blocked deep within you and cannot reach others. 'No-one appreciates all the work I do around here!' Her husband and children looked up in surprise. 'When's the last time I had five minutes of peace and quiet? It's all getting too much! I've had it!' And with those words, she stormed out of the house. *How had it come to this?* she wondered, as she walked through the nearby park. Deep down, she knew that this outburst had been coming for a while, but she had been trying to busy herself to avoid facing the truth. Something was missing. But then she stopped walking as another thought came to her. It was **her** who was missing. In the repetitive grind that was daily life, it felt like everything she did was for someone else, and she was barely keeping her head above water. She knew her outburst was unfair, because they didn't take her for granted. They all did little things that showed they wanted to help out, but she wasn't letting them. Her role used to make her feel important and needed, but now it just made her feel empty.

It's too easy to overlook how much you need the gift of your own attention. Always looking outward, it's hard to see yourself. Even when you do look within, the noisy chatter of grasping attention grabbers will drown out the quiet voice that tries to engage you in an exploration of who you really are and what you really want in life. Your attention must be allowed to wander deep within, because that voice will not be silenced. "Hiding from yourself" does not bury your yearnings, your fears or your vulnerabilities. Instead they seep into the flow of attention as regret, disappointment, blame or anger.

Being with people means first being with yourself. While others are nurtured by your role as parent, friend, boss or even passing stranger, ultimately it is the human being standing in your own skin who is most affected by the choices you make about where to give your attention. Let it push past the attention grabbers on the surface of your busy mind, just as a diver must plunge below the wild waves on the surface of the ocean. In the depths below are currents that will move you gently. Rather than fearing these depths and quickly returning to the surface, it is worth lingering there to get your bearings.

When you are comfortable in your own skin, this strong sense of self allows you to give more of your attention to others, asking nothing in return. 'I stopped off for a few minutes to drop my daughter for her play date after school, and had a brief chat with the other mum at the door. I didn't think more about it, but when I returned a few hours later, the mum came out and thanked me for helping her to make a big decision about a job opportunity that had been playing on her mind. I actually didn't give her any advice, but I think being able to listen fully had given her the space to hear herself more clearly.'

– WISE INVESTMENTS –

THE GIFT IS FOR GIVING > Giving attention to the things that give true meaning to life, frees the flow of attention from what has been diverting it, blocking it, or shattering it into fragments, and returns it to where it can do good again. You know you have given it wisely, when the things that are animated by attention's touch spread warmth in all directions.

Care is the currency we all need, if we are to thrive as individuals, families, communities, companies and countries. Attention is an investment in our collective wellbeing, a future built on support, encouragement, meaning, authenticity, strengths and loving connection. There is no more important question to ask yourself than, 'Where is my right attention now?' The answer will wake you up, and this is surely the first step to a full life.

9 Start with One Moment

A MATTER OF MOMENTS >

Life isn't a matter of milestones, but of moments.

ROSE KENNEDY, AUTHOR AND MATRIARCH OF THE KENNEDY POLITICAL DYNASTY, 1890 – 1995

While the flow of blood keeps your body living, it is the flow of clear, fresh attention that makes you feel alive. In its stream, it carries care, love, compassion, support, goodwill, wisdom and authenticity, and these things are desperately needed in our world today. Giving your attention generously, in any moment, breathes life into all that it touches, and this precious gift will grow as it passes from one person to the next.

'Are you having a bad day?' she asked the attendant behind the cash register, whose head was low and shoulders were slumped forward. But a short conversation between them triggered a burst of laughter, and she continued on her way through the shopping centre, with a spring in her step. Passing the same checkout on her return to the car park, she couldn't resist glancing over at the attendant. She was almost unrecognizable. The gift of attention, a moment of conversation and care, was still flowing through her. She was smiling and chatting with shoppers as they passed through her counter, and they were continuing on their way with a happy glow. Her investment of attention was finding its way into other people's minds, in the same way that the $20 note she had handed over may have ended up as change in their pockets.

Attention, the thread that connects you with life, weaves a tapestry that becomes the story of our world. Where attention flows freely and true connection is found, the colours are rich and vibrant, infused with hope, and revealing the very best of humanity. This world can be a work of beauty, if we all remember that there is only one tapestry and we write these stories together.

SAVE OUR ATTENTION > A threatened resource needs an urgent response. It's time to bring attention back from the brink of extinction and revive the dying art of paying attention. The loss of any precious resource has far-reaching effects, undermining all the broader systems that rely on it for their health. As a rainforest dies, it is not only the trees that disappear, but all the flora and fauna that reside within its canopy. And as attention dies, it is not just the simple ability to notice what's happening around you that fades. Attention sustains relationships, nourishes progress and maintains balance. We rely on it for advancement of meaningful, true happiness and a harmonious existence. The healthy flow of attention ripples between us, nourishing a healthy world. Don't let it wither and die without taking a stand, right here in this moment.

We need global action. That doesn't mean you must wait for someone to form the *Save Our Attention Foundation*, with strategies, meetings and campaigns. You don't need to rally in the streets, or garner political support. You don't need to wait until the famous people lend their name to raise awareness of attention's plight. You don't need to recite slogans or nail witty posters to the wall.

But you do need to make a donation.

DEPOSIT A MOMENT IN THE WORLD ATTENTION BANK > Imagine if even 1 percent of the people on this planet donated one moment of attention every day. Imagine how much difference a couple of million moments of pure attention could make. Smiles exchanged, fears released, help offered, gratitude expressed, food appreciated, love strengthened, dreams followed, solutions uncovered, excellence achieved, choices made, peace agreed. There is no limit to what a moment of attention can offer to our needy world.

Do you want to live in a world where attention flows freely and is given generously; a world where it is treasured as a precious resource to be invested wisely, rather than wasted; a world where we act to remove blockages, rather than build barriers; a world where children are taught the value of attention and shown how to strengthen it, deepen it and steer it well; a world where we do not pull back from the vibrancy that attention reveals, but return constantly to replenish ourselves and others?

Give one moment today:

One moment to yourself is clarifying, nourishing and revitalising.

One moment to another is reassuring, calming and enlivening.

One moment to maintain the flow of attention through us all is the answer to whatever you seek in life.

It doesn't matter where you start, as long as you start. It only takes one moment to make your choice, a conscious decision that attention is precious and deserves gentle treatment. It only takes one moment to make a pledge, a promise to yourself that you will keep attention alive and healthy. And it only takes one moment to bring your attention back to the present and send its animating force wherever it is needed most.

THE STARTING MOMENT > Only you can choose the best place to start, but don't spend too long waiting around for the "right" moment. Every moment is perfect, once you pay attention.

Bus Love

As soon as I heard about re-runs, I knew I was guilty of this habit. But I didn't fully realise how it was holding me back. I immediately thought about my bus trip home. Someone once asked me where a particular restaurant was along the route. I had travelled this same way for ten years, but I had no idea. That thirty minutes of my day was a blur. I spent the whole time re-running things that had happened at work, words that were critical, decisions that were unfair, tasks that didn't go to plan. No wonder I walked in the door at home feeling more stressed out and anxious than I did leaving work! The time I spend on that bus, that was my starting moment. Now I remain present. I look out the window and notice things, strike up conversations with strangers, observe the beauty in the world. Things changed immediately from the very first day. I arrived home relaxed, replenished, refilled and present for my family. The moments that used to be filled with negativity have been replaced with moments of inspiration. I get the best business ideas, and they seem to appear from nowhere. It's been a month now, and my bus trip home is a daily ritual that I will continue for the rest of my life.

GEORGE, AUSTRALIA

From Chaos to Calm

The concept of "attention is a gift" really hit home for me. Although I was probably withholding attention in many areas of my life, I immediately thought of the morning meeting I have with my work crew, before they go out on the road. It's a busy and chaotic time and everyone wants a piece of me. I realised that I was rarely listening to the person in front of me. While they were talking, I was looking around at what needed to be done and planning ahead. So that was the moment I chose to start with. I made a pledge to listen with full attention to every person who spoke to me during that meeting, and an amazing thing happened. The meeting felt like it slowed down. We began to get more done and it seemed more organised. I know the guys appreciated it, but the biggest benefit came back to me. Within a week, I found that my mind had slowed down and it was easier to focus throughout the whole day. I'd forgotten what it felt like to be so clear-headed.

MATT, AUSTRALIA

Serving the Servers

On the way home from the program, I stopped off at the petrol station. The checkout operator was almost through my payment, when I realised I hadn't even looked him in the eye. This was my moment! I got out of my busy head and connected with him by asking how his day was. He almost jumped. Despite having hundreds of people through the checkout that day, I suspect he was hardly noticed as a human being. Making the connection left both of us smiling. I thought I was already doing all of this, but I realised I was pretty selective. I would get in lifts without even making eye contact, or hop on the bus with more attention on the ticket machine than on the person behind it. So, from that day on, I've been more aware of giving the gift of attention to people I meet just for a moment. It didn't take me long to realise that I wasn't really giving "true" attention to my family. I was giving them focus with expectation of something in return, not just connecting the way I would with a stranger. So starting with strangers actually brought me closer to my family. I love it!

MARIE, FRANCE

Strengths First

When I was asked to give a presentation at the leaders' summit, I immediately felt the same old fears rise. Three hundred of my peers and bosses! What if I stuff up? Will I make a fool of myself? What will they think? All the reasons why I wasn't a good public speaker kept flashing through my mind. After a few minutes, I realised I was focusing on the wrong things. There must have been a reason I was asked

to do it. Others had confidence in me, so why was I withholding from myself? I decided in that moment that I would
stop focusing on all the things that could go wrong, and
start focusing on my strengths. I'd been through a process of
working out what they were, but hadn't really got around to
doing anything intentional to use them. This was the perfect
chance. Apparently I was engaging, could bring clarity to
any situation, and had a great sense of humour! It felt a bit
weird, but every time I got nervous or heard those voices in
my head trying to talk me out of it, I brought those strengths
to mind. It kept me calm, but it also helped me come up
with a presentation that was unlike what I normally would
have done. I thought it was way better, and the response
from the audience showed that they also agreed!

TRICIA, NEW ZEALAND

I'm Sorry

The statement "Withholding attention is a destructive act"
hit me hard. I had never really considered how damaging it
was, when I withheld attention. I sat down and wrote a list
of all the important relationships in my life, and identified
the three I felt that I was withholding from the most. It was
my husband, my child and one of my staff who I didn't get
along with. I had a conversation with each of them, because
I felt I needed to acknowledge it and say sorry. Those three
relationships came to life as soon as I stopped withholding.
There were particular times that I had been doing it most,
like when I walked in the door from work, or when I had a
client meeting coming up. I targeted those times to particularly give my attention generously. It worked so well that

I could feel it keep flowing even beyond those times. Such a simple act, but so powerful.

MIRIAM, USA

Trading Time

I was in a management team meeting and the President said, 'I think we need to have some staff team-building activities.' This was the best he could come up with, after spending an hour analysing the poor staff satisfaction results. I had only just returned from my seminar on attention, and it was blindingly obvious to me that we'd been missing the point. So I spoke up, which no-one ever does once the President has spoken! But I suggested that our staff don't want more time with us, they want our attention. I explained the difference: that more time would change very little, but quality attention would make them feel listened to and cared for, all the things that had rated so low. We had been too busy worrying about our company's future, and we hadn't been giving them our attention. When I looked around, the others were nodding. They had never thought about it like this, and neither had I before. But now we all knew this was the truth. Then the President surprised us all and said, 'Okay, then we're going to start it here, in these meetings. I want to know more about what you're all thinking from now on.' From that day on, lots of things have changed.

MIKE, ENGLAND

Email Ignorance

Sometimes I get so many emails that I just feel overwhelmed. So I start ignoring some, not bothering to reply. I had always done it on the basis that those ones were probably just trying to get something from me or sell me something. But I now realise that I was withholding attention when I did this. It doesn't show respect for the flow of attention, because I was acting like a blockage, and I know if it happens to me it doesn't feel good. So this is where I decided to start reviving attention. I now acknowledge every email, even if it is just two words, like "thank you". I found that it took next to no time and, rather than increasing the feeling of being overwhelmed, it was the opposite! I got things off my mind straight away, and it made me more disciplined with my whole emailing regime. It's so much easier to keep attention flowing than to resist it!

CATHERINE, AUSTRALIA

Sisterly Love

I now see why my younger sister would sometimes get tense with me. Growing up, we shared the same room. When I got to the teenage years where I needed my space, I would often ignore her. She wanted to play, but I would block her out by reading a book, or just avoid her. We continue to be good friends, but I can see the past still lives on, because she often thinks I'm not listening to her. So, rather than getting frustrated about it, I realised she was my starting moment, and I am extra vigilant when I am with her. I stop whatever I am doing and give full attention. No phones, no "other jobs to squeeze in", no watching mindless TV together. Our relationship is getting deeper, and I am pretty sure she has noticed my efforts.

BEATRICE, SWEDEN

Safe Switching

The nature of my work means that I am constantly dealing with interruptions. I can't avoid it, so I was pretty sceptical about how I was going to help my attention. But I started taking a moment to rest my attention in the space between the interruptions. Instead of dragging myself all over the place, I would let my attention consciously detach from one thing, then give it to the next. For example, when I am at the computer and someone comes to the door, as I turn my chair towards them, I am also turning my attention. It feels like gently redirecting a stream, and I even picture that sometimes. I have also told myself that everything that gets my attention deserves the respect of receiving the same quality of attention, no matter what the task. It's amazing how that has transformed the jobs I hated into ones that just happen without any bother. I feel a lot more productive, and I overheard someone say that I seem to be nicer lately!

PAUL, USA

Food Appreciation

I was often frustrated with my wife, because every time we sat down for the evening dinner she'd prepared, she would start asking things like, 'How is it? Do you need anything else? Maybe there's not enough salt. It's not exactly what I was trying to make.' After a busy day, sometimes the questions would annoy me. But then I saw it from her perspective. She had put love and attention into creating a beautiful meal for me night after night, and I wasn't returning the gift of that attention. In fact, the more she asked me, the more I would withhold attention from her. I saw that I was causing my own frustration by being so blind about what was really going on. That was my starting moment. I no longer scoff down the meal. I sit down with the intention to really taste it and experience the whole meal together. I started asking her questions about the flavours and how she had done something, and she was surprised, and maybe a little bit worried in the beginning. But we've settled into a really nice dinner routine now. Sometimes all I do is say, 'Beautiful dinner, honey.' But she is so much happier, and her little passing comments are no longer desperate pleas for acknowledgement. The surprising side effect is that it refreshes me from my day.

BRIAN, WALES

Withholding from Animals

I love my dog but, when I am busy, she is definitely the first one to suffer. I'm often too tired to walk her when I get home. Sometimes I just toss her food bowl down and get on with the day. Even when I do take her to the park, I tend to be distracted by my phone. One day she actually came up and knocked it out of my hand with her nose. That was a clear message and I thought: *It's not just people we withhold attention from, it's animals too.* So when I walk in at the end of the day, I let her draw me into the present. Animals are so good at that, and I make it a priority to fully connect with her. One moment of real connection with pats, hugs and looking into her eyes, helps me de-stress from the day, and it's clearly the highlight of her day. We both look forward to it. She's like an attention guide for me.

KATE, IRELAND

Drama Queen

The embarrassing fact is that I immediately identified with being an "attention thief". I was constantly texting or phoning people about my dramas. I have also been guilty of putting posts onto social media like "worst day ever!"—just to get a response. That stuff instantly gets twenty comments from friends, sending lovely messages and asking what happened. That used to validate me, but I now realise how selfish it is. Those twenty people were distracted, and for no good reason. My friends all have important work to do, and I know they care. I'm not sure if they realise I've stopped being an attention thief, but I actually feel really good about it, like I am protecting them.

ANGIE, USA

Ocean Appreciation

This might sound strange, but I have started giving one moment to nature. I love going to the beach, but when I am there I am often in my head. I have started looking out and really giving one moment in appreciation of the beautiful ocean I am swimming in, what it provides for the world, and for the species living in it. I am starting to appreciate and respect the environment a lot more now.

JOHN, AUSTRALIA

Savouring the Moment

Who would have thought that enjoying a simple a cup of tea could have such a dramatic effect? Well, it has for me! I used to rush from one thing to another: emails, requests, jobs to do all day long at work. And then when I got home,

I had notes from school, projects to organise, and extra-curricular activities to coordinate. It's hard being a single mum, and I have to admit I was struggling to stay on top of everything. I ended most days feeling like a failure. I rarely took a break for lunch, most of the time shovelling down my sandwich, while I paid some bills online. But one day I tried something different, and I stopped for a cup of tea. It changed my life. Not just the act of physically stopping, but the choice of mentally stopping. Taking one moment to really taste my cup of tea, rather than letting it disappear without even noticing! You would never believe what this single moment added to my life. For a start, my breathing would slow down and I could feel the stress leave my body. As my mind fell still, it would create the space for anything that needed to arise. I would see things with greater clarity, and sometimes it helped me rearrange my afternoon and achieve things better. I've introduced that moment of clarity into lots of things throughout the day. Sometimes it's the cup of tea, sometimes it's just sitting still for a moment and hearing the hum of the office, and sometimes it's using the walk from one room to the next as that moment to clear my mind. No matter what it is, that power of pausing has given me my life back.

Tracy, Australia

French Kiss

I was travelling to work on the train, but on this day I decided to "unplug". I realised that my commute was a blur, because I always listened to music. So I decided to just be present to what was going on around me. I quickly became aware of sobs coming from a seat near the door. A young woman was on the phone speaking in French to the person on the other end. I didn't know what she was saying, but one thing I knew for sure: she was distressed. In that moment of awareness, I reached into my bag and pulled out a small packet of tissues and just walked the few steps to her, placing it on her knee. She was still on the phone, but when she looked at me I just gave her a caring smile, and turned back to my seat. The young woman disembarked at the next stop, but she seemed a lot calmer now, and walked over and said, 'Merci, merci beaucoup.' That much French I understand! I won't know what that moment of attention really did for her, but the amazing thing was what it did for me. It completely filled me up. I went through the rest of the day with a very different approach to myself and to those around me.

SOFIE, AUSTRALIA

What's your starting moment? Where in your life is the most obvious need for attention? How can you revive your own attention and keep it flowing through the world? Where is your attention right now?

Join us and revive the dying art of paying attention. Visit:

www.mindgardener.com

References

Chapter 1

1 Gene Weingarten for *The Washington Post*, 'Forgetting a Child in the Back Seat of a Car is a Horrifying Mistake: Is it a Crime?' March 8, 2009

2 Killingsworth, M and Gilbert, Daniel T (2010), 'A Wandering Mind is an Unhappy Mind', *Science 12*, Vol 330, No 6006, p 932

3 Smallwood, J and Andews-Hanna J (2013), 'Not all minds that wander are lost: The importance of a balanced perspective on the mind-wandering state', *Frontiers in Psychology*, Vol 4, No 441

4 2008 Survey of 1000 people by Lloyds TSB Insurance

5 World Health Organisation Fact Sheet No 369, October 2012

Chapter 2

6 Cara Feinberg for *Harvard Magazine*, 'The Placebo Phenomenon', January, 2013

7 Daniel Goleman for *The New York Times*, 'Researchers Add Sounds of Silence to the Growing List of Health Risks', August 4, 1988

8   Joan L Luby, Deanna M Barch, Andy Belden, Michael S Gaffrey, Rebecca Tillman, Casey Babb, Tomoyuki Nishino, Hideo Suzuki and Kelly N Botteron (2012), 'Maternal Support in Early Childhood Predicts Larger Hippocampal Volumes at School Age', *Proceedings of the National Academy of Sciences,* Vol 109, No 8

9   Eisenberger, N and Lieberman, M with Williams, KD, 'Does Rejection Hurt? An FMRI Study of Social Exclusion', *Science,* Vol 302, No 5643, October 2003, pp 290–292

10 Donna St George for *The Washington Post,* 'Despite "Mummy Guilt", Time with Kids Increasing', March 20, 2007

11 Sorenson, Susan, 'How Employees' Strengths Make Your Company Stronger', *Gallup Business Journal,* 2014

12 Adam M. Grant, Elizabeth M. Campbell, Grace Chen, Keenan Cottone, David Lapedis and Karen Lee (2007), 'Impact and the art of motivation maintenance: The effects of contact with beneficiaries on persistence behaviour', *Organisational Behaviour and Human Decision Processes,* Vol 103, No 1

Chapter 3

13 Terrie E Moffitt, Louise Arseneault, Daniel Belsky, Nigel Dickson, Robert J Hancox, Hona Lee Harrington, Renate Houts, Richie Poulton, Brent W Roberts, Stephen Ross, Malcolm R Sears, W Murray Thomson, and Avshalom Caspi (2010), 'A Gradient of Childhood Self-Control Predicts Health, Wealth and Public Safety', *Proceedings of the National Academy of Sciences,* Vol 108, No 7

Chapter 4

14 Richard Alleyne for *The Telegraph,* 'Welcome to the Information Age: 174 Newspapers a Day', 11 February, 2011 and Short, James E, 'How Much Media?' *2013 Report on American Consumers*

15 Manhart, C, 'The Limits of Multitasking', *The Scientific American Mind,* 2004

16 Strayer, DL, Drews, FA and Crouch, DJ (2006), 'Comparing the Cellphone Driver and the Drunk Driver', *Human Factors,* 48, 381–391

– REFERENCES –

Chapter 5

17 Bob Sullivan and Hugh Thompson for *The New York Times*, 'Brain Interrupted', May 3, 2013

18 Seen on: www.alphadictionary.com

Chapter 6

19 Bolte Taylor, Jill (2009), 'My Stroke of Insight: A Brain Scientist's Personal Journey', Hodder Paperback

20 Sheehan, M and Pearse, S (2012), 'Wired for Life: Retrain Your Brain and Thrive', Hay House, Australia

21 Vivian Giang for *Fast Company*, 'How Everything We Tell Ourselves About How Busy We Are Is A Lie', September 5, 2014

Chapter 7

22 Stiles, J and Jernigan, T (2010), 'The Basics of Brain Development', *Neuropsychology Review*, 20 (4), pp 327–348

23 Wilson, TD, Reinhard, DA, Westgate, EC, Gilbert, DT, Ellerbeck, N, Hahn, C, Brown, CL and Shaked A, 'Just Think: The Challenges of the Disengaged Mind', *Science*, July 2014, Vol 345, No 6192, pp 75–77

24 Marc G Berman, Ethan Kross, Katherine M Krpan, Mary K Askren, Aleah Burson, Patricia J Deldin, Stephen Kaplan, Lindsey Sherdell, Ian H Gotlib and John Jonides, 'Interacting with Nature Improves Cognition and Affect for Individuals with Depression', *Journal of Affective Disorders*, 2012; Nov 140 (3), pp 300–305

25 Weistein N, Przybylski AK and Ryan R, 'Can Nature Make Us More Caring?', *Personality and Social Psychology Bulletin,* October 2009, Vol 35, No 10, pp 1315–1329

26 See reference list at *Center for Investigating Healthy Minds*: www.investigatinghealthyminds.org

Chapter 8

27 Post, SG (2005), 'Altruism, Happiness and Health: It's Good to be Good', *International Journal of Behavioural Medicine*, Vol 12, No 2, pp 66–77

28 Sara Konrath for *Psychology Today,* 'The Caring Cure: Can Helping Others Help Yourself?' August 29, 2013

29 Lim, C and Putnam, RD (2010), 'Religion, Social Networks, and Life Satisfaction', *American Sociological Review,* 75 (6), pp 914–933

30 Lyubomirsky, S (2008), 'The How of Happiness: The Scientific Approach to Getting the Life You Want', Penguin Press, New York

31 Fredrickson, B (2009), 'Positivity: Top-Notch Research Reveals the 3 to 1 Ratio That Will Change Your Life', Random House, New York

32 Heaphy, E and Losada, M, 'The Role of Positivity and Connectivity in the Performance of Business Teams: A Nonlinear Dynamics Model', *American Behavioral Scientist,* February 2004, Vol 47, pp 740–765

About Mind Gardener®

Everything you think, learn, see and do shapes your brain and changes your life. Whether you realise it or not, you've been training your brain since the day you were born. You are a mind gardener.

Martina Sheehan & Susan Pearse

Mind Gardener® was founded by Martina and Susan in 2009. It is a platform designed to *wake up the world.* Now, more than ever, it's time to let go, look up, and be present in your life.

MIND GARDENER® IN YOUR BUSINESS

Companies that succeed in the future will be those expert not in time management, but in attention management.

THOMAS H. DAVENPORT & JOHN C. BECK

The sad fact is that too many people are "switched off" at work, unable to give quality attention to the things that matter most. Through their award-winning Conscious Leadership Program, Martina and Susan have been showing leaders how to make attention management a new priority for their business, helping them to enhance the quality of decisions, generate true care for customers, boost productivity and create workplaces where employees experience a real sense of purpose and vitality. Conscious Leaders are awake to themselves, to their people and their customers, and to the ways their business can make a difference in the world.

MIND GARDENER® IN YOUR LIFE

The faculty of voluntarily bringing back a wandering attention, over and over again, is the very root of judgment, character, and will . . . An education which should improve this faculty would be the education par excellence.

WILLIAM JAMES

Martina and Susan are passionate about helping you revive the dying art of paying attention. It's the key to living a full and vibrant life, and without it, life's meaning fades. But they don't just talk about it; they have created a range of practical resources to guide people beyond inspiration to daily action. They know that "what you focus on grows", and their online programs, apps, step-by-step guides, workshops and retreats offer you a pathway to happiness, meaning, fulfilment and success. So, what are you cultivating? Because *you're* a mind gardener.

One Moment Please is Martina and Susan's second book published by Hay House. Their first book, *Wired for Life: Retrain Your Brain and Thrive,* explores the five fears that hold people back in work and in life, and it continues to inspire people to take meaningful steps to create the life they really want.

You can find more information at www.mindgardener.com.

About the Authors

SUSAN PEARSE

Susan Pearse will change the way you think. A quarter life crisis, a shopping trip to New York, and a chance meeting with His Holiness the Dalai Lama lead to the discovery of her life's purpose: to wake up the world. She swapped clothes shopping for spiritual shopping, exploring everything from quantum physics and neuroscience, to crystals and chakras. She found one core truth that she now teaches people in all walks of life: the need to get out of your head and fully connect with your life. Her passion is to teach people the power and skill of being in the present moment, in business and in life.

Susan is regularly called on by the media to share her tips for mindful living. She is a sought-after speaker, and writes for the Huffington Post. She is on the Development Board of the Queensland Brain Institute, a world leading organisation in brain research based in Australia.

As a working mother and entrepreneur, Susan understands the challenges of juggling a busy and rewarding career while maintaining a fulfilling family life. Susan lives in Brisbane with her husband, Jason, and children, Holly and Jack.

MARTINA SHEEHAN

Martina Sheehan is best known for opening people's eyes to the power of their mind. Whether it was just in her nature, or because of a near-death experience in her childhood, she has always sought to understand the deeper nature of things. Graduating from university with a degree in engineering was just the first step in her journey to discover what really makes us tick. She's very glad she never achieved her childhood dream of becoming an astronaut, realising it's the magic and mayhem on earth that still cries out for exploration and understanding. Instead, she's a pioneer at the final frontier: the human mind. Her great passion is to teach people the truth about the precious gift of attention.

Martina has run her own successful businesses for over fifteen years, and is a trusted guide for those who know it's time to live and work with deeper connection and greater purpose. She is renowned for finding the right tone to open the minds of leaders to deep truths often overlooked in the business world, and she is regularly invited to speak at conferences.

Martina lives in Brisbane with her husband, Phil. Together they created Work Bike Balance, a company that combines a love of travel, cycling, and attention fitness to deliver professional development programs to executives who are passionate about cycling.

Notes

Notes

Notes

Notes

Hay House titles of related interest:

YOU CAN HEAL YOUR LIFE, the movie,
starring Louise L. Hay & Friends
(available as a 1-DVD program and an expanded 2-DVD set)
Watch the trailer at: **www.LouiseHayMovie.com**

AMBITION to MEANING, the movie,
starring Dr. Wayne W. Dyer
(available as a 1-DVD program and an expanded 2-DVD set)
Watch the trailer at: **www.DyerMovie.com**

THE ART OF EXTREME SELF-CARE,
Transform Your Life One Moment at a Time
Cheryl Richardson

GETTING REAL ABOUT HAVING IT ALL,
Be Your Best, Love Your Career and Bring Back Your Sparkle
Megan Dalla-Camina

THE POWER OF INTENTION:
Learning to Co-create Your World, Your Way,
by Wayne Dyer

BREAKING THE HABIT OF BEING YOURSELF:
How to Lose Your Mind and Create a New One,
by Dr Joe Dispenza

E-SQUARED,
Nine Do-It-Youself Energy Experiments that Prove Your Thoughts
Create Your Reality,
by Pam Grout

WIRED FOR LIFE,
Retrain Your Brain and Thrive,
by Martina Sheehan & Susan Pearse

We hope you enjoyed this Hay House book. If you'd like to receive our online catalogue featuring additional information on Hay House books and products, or if you'd like to find out more about the Hay Foundation, please contact:

Hay House Australia Pty. Ltd.,
18/36 Ralph St., Alexandria NSW 2015
Phone: +61 2 9669 4299 • *Fax:* +61 2 9669 4144
www.hayhouse.com.au

Published and distributed in the USA by:
Hay House, Inc., P.O. Box 5100, Carlsbad, CA 92018-5100
Phone: (760) 431-7695 • *Fax:* (760) 431-6948
www.hayhouse.com®

Published and distributed in the United Kingdom by:
Hay House UK, Ltd., Astley House, 33 Notting Hill Gate,
London, W11 3JQ • Phone: 44-203-675-2450
Fax: 44-203-675-2451 • www.hayhouse.co.uk

Published and distributed in the Republic of South Africa by:
Hay House SA (Pty), Ltd., P.O. Box 990, Witkoppen 2068
Phone/Fax: 27-11-467-8904
www.hayhouse.co.za

Published in India by:
Hay House Publishers India, Muskaan Complex, Plot No. 3, B-2,
Vasant Kunj, New Delhi 110 070
Phone: 91-11-4176-1620 • *Fax:* 91-11-4176-1630
www.hayhouse.co.in

Distributed in Canada by:
Raincoast, 9050 Shaughnessy St., Vancouver, B.C. V6P 6E5
Phone: (604) 323-7100 • *Fax:* (604) 323-2600
www.raincoast.com

Take Your Soul on a Vacation
Visit www.HealYourLife.com® to regroup, recharge, and reconnect with your own magnificence. Featuring blogs, mind-body-spirit news, and life-changing wisdom from Louise Hay and friends.

Visit www.HealYourLife.com® today!

CPSIA information can be obtained
at www.ICGtesting.com
Printed in the USA
LVHW040824050623
748888LV00002B/86

9 781401 938659